Cooking Triumphs
of a Tightwad

To Kathryn

Don Dunnam

Cooking Triumphs of a Tightwad

Don Dunnam

VANTAGE PRESS
New York

The recipes contained in this book have been selected and written down by the author.

Recipes herein have not been tested by the publisher.

FIRST EDITION

Published by Vantage Press, Inc.
516 West 34th Street, New York, New York 10001

Manufactured in the United States of America
ISBN: 0-533-12772-6

Library of Congress Catalog Card No.: 98-90374

0 9 8 7 6 5 4 3 2 1

To Richard, for his testing and encouragement, and to Kailey and Doug, for their love and support

Contents

Soups, Sauces, Sandwiches, and Gravy

Kitchen Tips

Introduction

Hello. My name is Don Dunnam. I live in Sioux Falls, South Dakota, and I am a single parent with a partner and a near teenage daughter. They are my world, so I am sure you will read about my daughter often throughout this book.

I grew up in a family that was just at the poverty level or barely above. We all lived together in a house in the country. My mother, grandfather, grandmother, great-grandmother, aunt, uncle, three cousins, and me. We called our great-grandmother "Granny" and our grandmother "Grandma" to keep things straight. God, how I hated that television show "The Waltons."

My great-grandmother was very Swedish. She and I could talk for hours about nothing in particular. The rest of the family had some difficulty with her because she was never afraid to give her opinion. It didn't matter if it was good, bad, or none of her business, you got it anyway. One thing the entire family had to agree about her, though: She was a wonderful cook.

I remember sitting in the kitchen with her for many hours, peeling the year's harvest of apples from the apple trees. There were apple pies everywhere cooling, apple bread, apple cookies, and apple butter. Then the garden was harvested: tomato soup, tomato sauce, catsup, potato pancakes, potato soup, canned beans, canned carrots, canned pickles, canned pumpkin, pumpkin pies, and the list goes on. It usually took a little more than a week to finish all of these and get them into the freezer and the "cellar." Of course we would have to eat what didn't fit into the freezer. I know. It was a tough job.

Granny and I would talk about her previous marriages and her Swedish parents while we were cutting, chopping, peeling (bleeding), and boiling. She was the only person with whom I shared my hopes for the future. The rest of the family was always too busy whining about how bad they had it and never once gave a thought about how to improve their own lives. My grandfather called it PMS—Poor Me Syndrome.

I hadn't realized that in the many days and hours I was spending with Granny, I was also learning her technique for cooking. She always made the most wonderful meals out of what was available. Granny once asked me to take my BB gun outside and get her a couple of crows for dinner. I did manage to shoot one, but after that bird hit the ground, I have refused to kill another living thing the rest of my life. My grandfather went out and got a couple more. We had crow pie (like chicken pot pie) for dinner.

Later in life, and after Granny had passed on, I was married for seven years. I did a lot of cooking, but it wasn't until after I divorced that I wanted to become more than just adequate. I received joint custody of my daughter. (On paper anyway.) It turned out that my daughter spends most of her time with my partner and me. So, with a very closed budget and an open mind, I set out to do as my family had done—do the best with what you have.

Now some people think that I am "cheap" when it comes to grocery shopping. Maybe I am. I prefer "frugal." As long as the food tastes great, why not use that little extra grocery money somewhere else? My grocery bill is between $40 and $50 a week for three people and the occasional guest(s). My mother and I have been trading off on making the Thanksgiving and Christmas dinner. For twelve people, drinks, appetizers, dinner, and desserts, I spend between $80 and $120.

One evening, I was at home in our small apartment cooking for ourselves and our friends. I normally tell my ingredients to my guests *only when they ask.* After telling them of the ingredients I use for what they were calling a "wonderful" meal, I heard, "You should really make your own cookbook." After many months of pondering, I finally decided to try my hand at it.

I should mention that most times I do not like to spend a lot of time in the kitchen. Therefore, most of these recipes are fast but make people think that you have spent all day cooking. Most of these recipes are recipes that were given to me by my friends and family. I have changed the ingredients to be less costly and sometimes even taste better. A couple of the recipes, I created myself.

The serving sizes of the recipes vary. I have always wondered why a recipe might say they range from four to six servings or something like that. When I was putting this book together, I think that I discovered why. Some people eat little bird bite servings that constitute a serving (if not a half serving). Other people can eat enough for three. You really have think about your guest's eating habits when trying to decide how much of the recipe that you have to make.

I did not include any pictures of the food in this book because I thought the lack of pictures would go along well with the topic of generic products. And in my opinion, pictures in a cook book are like pictures on a menu in a restaurant. They are nice to look at, but when you actually get the food, it rarely ever looks like what you ordered. If you do not cook a lot anyway, why set yourself up for the disappointment of your food not looking like what is pictured in a book even though it may taste the same?

First Things First

Set up your kitchen. In most recipes you do need the special ingredient to give the recipe that just right flavor, and it usually is just one ingredient. Most everything else within the dish can be substituted with a **GENERIC** or store brand equivalent and still taste great. Surprisingly, most of the "special ingredients" in a recipe are the spices themselves. Most grocery stores now carry spices in small generic containers that cost less than a dollar. Whenever I need to do some shopping, I pick up a spice or two, even if I have no idea what it is. Another way to find spices and herbs is to watch "crazy days" sales at department stores.

You will notice that I use garlic powder instead of garlic cloves in the recipes. I do this because I have found that if I buy clove garlic, it sits on the shelf and turns bad before I have a chance to use them again. **(1/8 teaspoon garlic powder is equal to one clove of garlic.)**

A lot of recipes call for broth of one form or another. I have found when working with little time and a limited budget, bouillon cubes work wonders. You can purchase these in either generic or store brands. This is also offered in a ground powder form, but personally I prefer the cubes because they are easier to measure and have a less grainy texture.

I always have about four or five cans each of tomato paste and tomato sauce in the kitchen—also generic. The flavor you might think that could be lost can be replaced by additional spices.

Hamburger and chicken. As you well know, the prices of meat goes up and down like a yo-yo. I buy hamburger by the family pack and then I cut it down into individual one pound squares, wrap each in plastic wrap, put them in the freezer, and defrost what I need. I heard a friend say that she could not afford to buy the family pack. She doesn't realize that a lot of times it is less expensive dividing it that way, than to buy them by the pound. Sure each square may not be exactly a pound, but who is going to measure your food?

I buy boneless chicken breasts because they are fast and easy to cook. Even though they are usually a little more expensive than to buy them with bones. In the colder months, I still buy the boneless chicken breasts. However I also get a whole chicken or two and chicken parts. This way I can use the oven and turn the thermostat down while cooking, saving even more.

What about vinegar and oils? I have a gallon bottle of distilled white vinegar that you can buy in the generic or store brand for usually under two dollars. I use it for salad dressings and other recipes that call for vinegar. Not to mention how vinegar and newspaper do a fantastic job in cleaning the windows. I use a vegetable oil for basically all recipes where it calls for olive oil or any other form of oil. Again it is inexpensive and can be bought in a generic or store brand.

When I want to add vegetables to the meal menu, I just open a can of vegetables and add a couple of tablespoons of real butter for flavor. Real butter is more expensive than margarine, but then again you can buy store brands of the real butter and add taste to any meal.

I have always had the problem of buying a bunch of carrots, celery, or other vegetables, use what I needed, and having the rest sit in the vegetable bin in the refrigerator and rotting. Then I discovered that some grocery stores, usually in the deli section, have vegetables already peeled, cut and cleaned in small bags ready to use. Of course this calls for a little planning ahead, but I buy these bags of mixed vegetables when I am planning a stew, roasted meat, or soup of some kind. Don't tell anyone else about this, though, because your friends and family will think that you spent all day preparing the meal for them. A good meal does have its perks sometimes.

Garnish is nice to include when making a meal for company or just to make your family feel special. This can be done by using a lemon slice placed on the edge of the plate with a small sprig of parsley in the center. Or when I had no parsley, I have used the leaves from the tops of celery stalks and placed them together with thin carrot slices that you get when you use a potato peeler. Another idea is using a green onion, take the tip of a paring knife and shred the white portion of the onion; down to the ends. Be careful not to cut the strips off. Soak the onion in cold water in the refrigerator. After a couple of hours, the onion will bloom like a flower. The important thing with garnish is to use your own imagination and have fun with it. Of course you don't want a plate that is all garnish with no food.

Over all, for almost any of the ingredients in the recipes in this book, you can use a generic or store brand: cream cheese, any kind of nut, any kind of graham cracker pie crust (other pie crusts should be made from scratch because it adds to the whole flavor), popcorn, syrups, rice, and the list goes on and on. Besides, the money saved on these ingredients will more than make up for splurging on one or two special ingredients to get just the right flavor for a dish. The most important thing is to experiment and have fun. I have had some failures also, but they were still learning experiences. "*If at first you don't succeed . . .* " try again or order pizza.

Cooking Triumphs
of a Tightwad

Appetizers and
Beverages

Stuffed Mushrooms

This is a very good recipe for parties where you plan on serving the appetizers. I say that because these mushrooms cook fast, cool down fast, and get eaten fast. Do not use canned mushrooms for this one. However, generic sour cream works well.

8 oz Mushrooms Whole
1 tablespoon Butter
2 tablespoons chopped Green
  Onion

2 tablespoons dry Bread
  Crumbs
2 tablespoons Sour Cream
dash Salt and dash Pepper

Remove stems from mushrooms and set aside the caps. Finely chop the stems. In a small bowl, mix the stems, butter and green onion and microwave for 1 to 1 1/2 minutes on high. Remove from microwave and add the remaining ingredients. Spoon into the mushroom caps and arrange in a circle on the outside edge of a microwave safe plate with the filling side up. Microwave two to three minutes until hot and serve.

Pickled Mushrooms

This is a very good appetizer for a Christmas, New Year's Eve, or Super Bowl party. The red wine vinegar is the flavor to this recipe. Because of this, I substitute canned mushrooms in this recipe. This recipe looks great in a silver or decorated glass serving dish.

1/3 cup Red Wine Vinegar
1 small Onion
2 teaspoons Parsley Flakes
1 tablespoon Brown Sugar
1/3 cup Salad Oil

1 teaspoon Salt
1 teaspoon Prepared Mustard
2 6-oz cans of Mushroom
  Crowns

In a small saucepan, combine vinegar, salad oil, the onion thinly sliced and separated into rings, salt, parsley, mustard, and brown sugar. Bring to a boil. Drain the mushrooms, then add them to the heated mixture, and simmer for five to six minutes. Chill in a covered bowl for several hours, stirring occasionally. Drain the liquid off just before serving.

Bacon Cheddar Puffs

This appetizer I like to make and serve next to the pickled mushrooms. Besides their looking and smelling great, the real butter enhances the flavor and you will need to double or triple the recipe when serving more than five guests.

1/2 cup Milk
2 tablespoons Butter
1/2 cup Flour
2 Eggs
1/2 cup shredded Cheddar
  Cheese

4 Bacon slices, cooked and
  crumbled
1/4 cup chopped Green On-
  ion
1/4 teaspoon Garlic Salt
1/4 teaspoon Pepper

Preheat your oven to 350 degrees. Bring the milk and butter to a boil over a medium heat. Remove from heat and add the flour until the mixture forms a ball and leaves the sides of the pan. Add remaining ingredients, stirring until the mixture is smooth. Using a teaspoon, drop onto a greased cookie sheet. Bake for twenty-five minutes or until puffed and golden brown.

Cheese Ball

Everyone seems to have a cheese ball recipe. I have tried a few different ones, but this is the one that I seem to like the best. I place the ball in the center of a decorative plate and surround it with different types of crackers.

2 8-oz Cream Cheese—softened
1 8-oz shredded Cheddar Cheese
2 teaspoons Worcestershire Sauce
1 teaspoon Lemon Juice
1/2 cup Almonds—slivered
dash of Cayenne Pepper

Mix together the cream cheese and the cheddar cheese until well blended. Add the remaining ingredients and again mix well. Place a piece of wax paper on the table and spread the almonds out in a single layer. With your hands, roll the cheese mixture into a ball. Roll in the almonds, trying to pick up as many of the nuts as will collect on the ball. Carefully wrap in plastic wrap and refrigerate for several hours. (I make this the day before I am going to use it.) When ready to serve, remove from the refrigerator and roll in your hands to get the ball shape back. Unwrap and serve.

Mini Pizzas

This makes a great television snack without your having to buy the mini pizzas from your local grocer. All items in this recipe can be generic and still add up to a great taste.

1 pound Ground Beef
1/4 teaspoon Garlic Powder
2 cans Tomato Paste
1/2 cup Parmesan Cheese
2 teaspoons Oregano

2 packages Refrigerated Biscuits
1 cup American Cheese, shredded

Preheat the oven to 425 degrees. Brown the ground beef. Add the oregano and garlic and simmer for ten minutes. Drain. On a greased cookie sheet, flatten biscuits to form 4" circles, using a floured custard cup or coffee cup. Let the dough come out around what you are using to flatten the dough to form the edge of the crust. Make six crusts per cookie sheet. Fill each with a tablespoon of tomato paste and then the hamburger mixture. Sprinkle with the American cheese and then the parmesan cheese. Bake for ten minutes and serve.

Another way for a fast pizza snack is as follows. Divide English muffins in half and place with the cut portion up. Top with a tablespoon of pizza sauce and your favorite toppings. Put the mozzarella on last. Bake at 400 degrees for ten minutes. If you use wheat muffins and low fat ingredients, you can make a "healthy" snack and completely fool the kids.

Rainbow Jello

Here is another one that is really a hit with the kids, besides being just a cheery snack.

6 8-oz Jello packs (1 each—   9" x 13" cake pan
    grape, blue raspberry, lime,
    lemon, orange, cherry)

Start with the Grape Jello. Add 1 1/2 cups boiling water and stir until dissolved. Pour into the cake pan and place on a level shelf in the refrigerator for thirty minutes. When you place the pan in the refrigerator, immediately start to boil the next 1 1/2 cups water and make the Blue Raspberry Jello. This will allow the water to cool slightly. After the thirty minutes, pour on top of the grape layer. Repeat the process with the next layers, lime, lemon, orange, and cherry. Refrigerate after the final layer for at least one hour. Dip a table knife in hot water and cut the jello into rectangles. Shake out of pan on to wax paper and then place on serving plate.

Hot Apple Cider

This is a very sweet apple cider. If you are planning on having guests, this is a nice drink to make just for the wonderful aroma that spreads throughout your house. On each cup served, I like to garnish with an apple wedge on the edge of the cup and a cinnamon stick in the cider.

1 gallon Apple Cider   1/2 cup Cinnamon Candies

Heat the apple cider and candies through in a large pan. Let the cider simmer over low heat for at least an hour before your guests arrive. Your whole house will fill with the smell of apples and cinnamon.

Virgin Coladas

1 8-oz Piña Colada Yogurt
1 tablespoon Honey

1 8-oz can crushed Pineapple
4 Ice Cubes

Mix all ingredients together in a blender until smooth. Of course, this recipe yields wonderful Piña Coladas when you add about two shots of rum.

Hawaiian Punch(ed)

This is a fun punch for a summer or fall party. There is not much of a taste of alcohol in this punch, so keep the children away and make sure the bigger kids leave the keys at the door.

1 liter Coconut Rum
2 2-liter bottles Lemon-Lime
  Soda

1 liter Peach Schnapps
2 Hawaiian Punch, frozen
  concentrate

Thaw Hawaiian Punch and mix all ingredients together. Float your favorite fruit combination in the punch and serve. I like to use peaches and strawberries.

Breads

Banana Nut Bread

1 3/4 cup Flour
1/2 teaspoon Baking Soda
1/3 cup Butter
2 tablespoons Milk
1/4 cup chopped Nuts

1 1/4 teaspoons Baking Powder
2/3 cup Sugar
2 Eggs
2 ripe, mashed Bananas

Preheat oven to 350 degrees. Mix the flour, baking powder, baking soda, and sugar together. Add all remaining ingredients and blend well. Grease and flour one large OR two small loaf pans. Bake sixty to sixty-five minutes for large loaf pan or forty to forty-five minutes for small loaf pans, until a knife inserted in the center comes out dry.

Granola Bread

I do not know about you, but I love the smell of fresh-baked bread. I do not like the time it takes to make it if you have to use yeast, however. I substituted a granola cereal and baking powder for the yeast and came up with this recipe. I serve it hot with a meal or by itself just as a treat. It never lasts long enough to cool down.

3 cups Flour
4 teaspoons Baking Powder
1 Egg
2 tablespoons Oil

1 cup Sugar
1 1/2 teaspoons Salt
1 1/2 cups Milk
1 cup Granola Cereal

Heat oven to 350 degrees. In a large mixing bowl, stir together the flour, sugar, baking powder, and salt. Mix in the egg, milk, and oil. Gently stir in the granola cereal. Pour into a greased 9x5x3 inch bread pan. Bake for 1 to 1 1/4 hours until a toothpick inserted in the center comes out clean. Remove from pan and cool slightly on a wire rack.

Peanut Butter Cup Bread

If you are the type of person who likes to make baked gifts to give away for the holidays, this is a great recipe for that. It is very different, easy, and your friends will love it.

Mini Loaf Pans (5 x 2 1/2 x 2 inch)
3/4 cup Peanut Butter- smooth
1 Egg
1 teaspoon Vanilla
2 teaspoons Baking Powder
3/4 cup Chocolate Chips
1/2 cup Sugar
1 cup Milk
2 cups Flour
1/2 teaspoon Salt

Heat oven to 350 degrees. In a large bowl or mixer, blend together the peanut butter, sugar, egg, milk, and vanilla. Mix in the flour, baking powder, and salt. Once completely mixed, stir in the chocolate chips. Lightly grease four mini loaf pans. Fill each pan to 1/2 to 3/4 full. Bake for twenty-eight to thirty minutes or until a toothpick comes out clean. Cool completely on a wire rack. Dust with powdered sugar.

Doughnuts

These doughnuts do not use yeast, so the cooking time is cut in half. They are very good and do not last very long if there are kids around. Okay, if I am around.

2 Eggs
2 tablespoons Butter—melted
4 teaspoons Baking Powder
1/2 teaspoon Cinnamon
1 cup Milk

1 cup Sugar
4 cups Flour
1/4 teaspoon Salt
1/2 teaspoon Nutmeg

Beat eggs together until light and creamy. Add the sugar and the butter and blend well. Shift in all remaining ingredients and mix well. Begin heating the oil to fry the doughnuts. Roll the dough out on a lightly floured surface to about 1/4" thick. Cut with a floured doughnut cutter and fry a few at a time in hot oil. (I still do not have a doughnut cutter. I would not use it enough to see going out and buying one. I use the rim of a floured drinking glass and then the tube of a meat baster for the center hole.) Turn the doughnuts once while cooking. Drain on paper towels. (I put a mixture of sugar and cinnamon in a brown paper bag and drop the doughnuts in the bag as soon as I take them out of the oil. The bag soaks up some of the oil while coating the doughnuts with the sugar mixture.) Shake well. This will make about two dozen doughnuts.

Pie Pastry

This is my favorite pastry recipe for any kind of pie. It is very flaky and light and makes an apple pie simply wonderful. Yes, it does take some time to make this pastry, but the time is well worth the effort.

2 cups Flour
2 tablespoons Vegetable Oil
6 tablespoons Butter

8 to 10 tablespoons cold Water

Pour the flour into a large mixing bowl and add the oil. Blend in just enough cold water to make a firm dough. Knead the dough with your hands lightly until smooth. On a floured work surface, roll out the dough to a rectangle of about 6"x15". Cut two tablespoons of the butter into small pieces and place on top of the dough. Fold the dough into thirds, put in a plastic bag, and place in the refrigerator for fifteen minutes. Place the cold dough on your floured work surface with the open edge of the dough toward you. Roll out to the same size rectangle as before. Cut two more tablespoons of butter on top of the dough again. Fold again into thirds and place back into the refrigerator for fifteen minutes. Repeat as before with the last two tablespoons of butter. After the last fifteen minutes, cut the dough in half and roll into a disk shape. Place into your desired pie pan.

Basic Drop Biscuits

Experiment with this recipe. I have added a 1/2 cup shredded cheese and two teaspoons of chives to this recipe and they come out great. I have browned some diced onion in a pan with melted butter, drained completely, and added to the recipe to make onion biscuits also. Enjoy.

2 cups Flour
1/2 teaspoon Salt
1 cup Milk

3 teaspoons Baking Powder
1/3 cup Butter—melted

Heat oven to 450 degrees. Mix together all ingredients and drop from a teaspoon onto a greased cookie sheet. Bake for ten to twelve minutes. This will make a dozen biscuits.

Lemon Biscuits

This recipe will make about twenty biscuits and is really nice if you have a guest over for tea in the afternoon. They are also great with any fish meal.

4 cups Flour
1 1/2 teaspoon Baking Soda
2/3 cup Butter—softened
1 cup Milk

1/4 cup Sugar
1 teaspoon Salt
6 tablespoons Lemon Juice

Heat oven to 450 degrees. Mix together all of the dry ingredients: flour, sugar, baking soda, and salt. Cut in the butter and then add the lemon juice and milk. Mix quickly so that the milk does not sour. Knead on a lightly floured surface. Use a rolling pin, roll out to 1/2" thick, and then cut with a floured cutter. Place the biscuits on a lightly greased cookie sheet and bake for fifteen minutes.

Autumn Pancakes

1 cup Flour
2 tablespoons Sugar
1 Egg
1/4 teaspoon Nutmeg
2 tablespoons Oil

2 tablespoons Baking Powder
1/2 teaspoon Salt
1/4 teaspoon Cinnamon
1/8 teaspoon Ground Cloves

Heat a griddle or large pan to very hot. Mix all ingredients together. I use a soup serving spoon to keep all the pancakes about the same size. Brown on both sides and serve with warm syrup. **Apple Pancakes**: Melt two tablespoons of butter in a small frying pan. Add one apple that has been peeled, cored, and diced. Sauté until tender. Substitute the apple mixture for the oil before cooking the pancakes.

Tropical Syrup

This recipe makes about six servings, so you may want to make this for a large family or breakfast guests. It is a great change of pace for pancakes or waffles.

1 8-oz can Pineapple Chunks
1 tablespoon Cornstarch
1 Orange

2 6-oz cans Pine-Orange-
    Banana Juice
1 Banana
1 cup seedless Grapes

Drain the juice from the pineapple chunks into a saucepan. Stir in the pine-orange-banana juice. In a measuring cup, mix a tablespoon of the juice and the cornstarch together until smooth. Pour into the saucepan. Bring the mixture to a boil and cook for three minutes, stirring constantly. Let the mixture cool to almost room temperature. In a large bowl, place the pineapple, peel and slice the banana, and peel and slice the orange. Add the grapes. Stir the juice mixture over the fruit and then spoon over pancakes.

Honey Butter

2 cups Butter

1/4 cup Honey

Whip the butter until smooth. Add the honey and re-whip. If you save your plastic margarine containers, you can store your butter in one of those in the refrigerator. My daughter likes this on pancakes, bread, toast, etc.

Cajun Flavored Butter

As I have mentioned before, I like spicy food. I am the only one in my household who likes this recipe. Therefore, I make it just for myself when we have corn on the cob. The flavors together enhance any meal.

1/4 teaspoon Chili Powder
1/8 teaspoon Red Pepper
2 tablespoons Butter

1/4 cup Chicken Broth (1/4 water & 1/2 chicken bouillon cube)
1/4 teaspoon Black Pepper
1/8 teaspoon Garlic Powder
1 teaspoon Cornstarch

Melt the butter in the saucepan. Add the chili powder, black pepper, red pepper, and garlic powder. Cook over medium heat for one minute. Mix the cornstarch in with the broth until completely smooth, then pour in with the butter mixture. Cook over medium heat until thickened and then cook for two minutes more. Cool slightly and serve.

Cookies
and
Cakes

Monster Cookie Sandwiches

This recipe makes six sandwiches and is a great after-dinner dessert and fun for children's birthday parties.

3/4 tablespoon White Corn Syrup
1/2 cup Butter
1 cup Sugar
1/2 cup Peanut Butter
1 6-oz package M & M's

1 quart Vanilla Ice Cream, softened
3 Eggs
1/2 cup packed Brown Sugar
2 teaspoons Baking Soda
1 6-oz package Chocolate Chips
4 1/2 cups Oatmeal

Preheat your oven to 350 degrees. Mix all ingredients together in a large bowl, except for the ice cream. Use an ice cream scoop and place a scoop of dough on a large, greased cookie sheet. Only two at a time. Flatten with a large spatula. Bake for ten to twelve minutes, making sure to get golden brown but not too crispy. Cool for ten minutes on the cookie sheet before removing. Cool on a wire rack or plastic sheet. When the cookies are completely cooled, tip one upside down and place a scoop of ice cream on it. Spread lightly with a butter knife. Place another cookie on top right side up and gently press them together so the ice cream comes to the edge. Smooth the ice cream from the edge all the way around with the back of the knife. Wrap each sandwich in plastic wrap and place in the freezer. Freeze for at least two hours before eating.

Hamburger Cookies

While taking a speaking and writing course in college, we were given an assignment to do a demonstration speech. A majority of the class spoke on cooking one thing or another. This recipe is from another student who makes these as a project to do with his young daughter. I thought they were a lot of fun to make, a lot of fun to look at, not to mention how much fun they are to eat.

3 boxes Vanilla Wafers
3 cups Powdered Sugar
1/4 cup Milk
1 teaspoon Peppermint Extract or Vanilla
Green Food Coloring

1 package Chocolate Sandwich Cookies
1/2 cup Butter
1/4 teaspoon Salt
Red Food Coloring

Using an electric mixer, blend the powdered sugar, butter, milk, salt and extract into a frosting. Divide the frosting in half, placing in two bowls. Drop about ten drops of green food coloring into one half of the frosting, and then place ten drops of red food coloring into the other half. Blend well. Twist apart the chocolate sandwich cookies. Using a table knife, spread about 1/2 tablespoon green frosting on one half of the chocolate cookie and then spread the same amount of red frosting on the other side. Place a vanilla wafer on each side of the chocolate cookie with the flat side of the wafer toward the frosting. Squeeze together so the frosting shows around the edges. The vanilla wafers represent the hamburger bun, the green frosting is the lettuce, the white frosting filling of the chocolate sandwich cookie is the mayonnaise, the chocolate cookie is the hamburger, and the red frosting is the tomato. Enjoy.

Rainbow Cookies

I made these cookies for a bake sale and they sold very fast. Adults kept buying them "to take home to their kids," and kids just simply love them. They do take time to prepare, but the compliments you will receive will be well worth the effort.

8 tablespoons Butter
2 Egg Yolks
1 teaspoon Baking Powder
6 tablespoons Milk

Food Coloring—Red, Green,
    Yellow, Blue
1 cup Sugar
3 1/4 cups Flour
1/4 teaspoon Salt
1/2 teaspoon Anise Oil

Mix together the butter and sugar thoroughly. Mix in the egg yolks. Add the remaining ingredients, except the food coloring and blend well. Divide the dough into four equal portions. Blend a separate food coloring into each of the portions. Place a sheet of wax paper on your working surface and roll blue dough out into a rectangle, making it almost 1/2" thick. On a separate sheet of wax paper, roll out the green dough to the same dimensions. Flip on top of the blue dough. Repeat for the red dough and yellow dough, piling on top of the blue dough. Start with a short edge of the rectangles, using the wax paper to help form the dough, and roll the dough jelly roll style. Moisten the end edge of dough with a little water and seal. Wrap the dough in plastic wrap and place in the refrigerator for at least three hours. Turn the dough occasionally to keep round. Heat oven to 375 degrees. Cut the cookies to about 1/8" thick and place on a well-greased cookie sheet. Bake for ten minutes. While the cookies are baking, place remaining dough back in the refrigerator. This will make about fifty cookies.

Sugar Cookies

My daughter and I make these over the holiday season. The real butter and powdered sugar make these cookies simply mouth-watering.

2/3 cup Butter
1 teaspoon Vanilla
4 teaspoons Milk
1 1/2 teaspoons Baking Pow-
    der

3/4 cup Powdered Sugar
1 Egg
2 cups Flour
1/4 teaspoon Salt

Cream together the butter, powdered sugar, and vanilla. Add the egg and beat until fluffy. Blend in the remaining ingredients. Divide the dough in half and chill both for one hour. Preheat oven to 375 degrees. Work with one half at a time. Roll thin on a floured surface and cut into shapes or use a glass to cut circles. Place on greased cookie sheet and sprinkle with sugar or colored sugar. Bake for about seven minutes. Cool completely before decorating.

Oatmeal Cookies

1 cup melted Butter
2 Eggs
1 1/2 teaspoons Lemon Juice
1 teaspoon Flour
1 teaspoon Baking Powder
1 teaspoon Cinnamon
3 cups Oatmeal

1 1/2 cups packed Brown
    Sugar
1/2 cup Milk
1 3/4 cups Flour
1 teaspoon Baking Soda
1 teaspoon Salt
1 teaspoon Nutmeg
1 cup Raisins

Preheat oven to 400 degrees. Blend together the butter, brown sugar, eggs, milk, and lemon juice. Add remaining ingredients and mix well. Drop dough by tablespoons full on to a greased cookie sheet and bake for about eight minutes.

Rum Balls

Not necessarily for the children. Just the children at heart.

3 cups Vanilla Wafer crumbs
(about 100 cookies)
1/2 cup Dark Rum

4 cups ground Walnuts
1/2 cup Honey
Powdered Sugar

Combine all ingredients, except for the powdered sugar. Shape into balls about 1". Roll in the powdered sugar and store in a tightly covered container.

Snicker Bars

2 1/2 cups Chocolate Chips
1/4 cup Milk
1/2 cup chunky Peanut Butter
1 teaspoon Vanilla
40 Caramels

1 cup Sugar
1/4 cup Butter
1 cup Marshmallow Cream
1 cup Peanuts
2 tablespoons Water

In a saucepan over low heat, melt 1 cup of the chocolate chips. Put into a greased 9" x 13" baking pan. Place into the freezer until firm. Boil the sugar, milk, and butter for five minutes. Add 1/4 cup of the peanut butter, the marshmallow cream, and the vanilla. Pour into the pan on top of the chocolate layer. Sprinkle with remaining peanuts and cool. Melt the caramels in with the water. Pour over the top of the peanuts. Melt the remaining chocolate chips and peanut butter over low heat. Pour on top as the last layer and refrigerate overnight. Before cutting, let the bars come to room temperature for one hour. Cut with a sharp knife dipped in boiling water.

Pecan Pie Brownies

Topping
1/4 cup Butter
3/4 cup firmly packed Brown
  Sugar
1 teaspoon Vanilla
2 tablespoons Flour
2 Eggs
2 cups chopped Pecans

Brownies
1 cup Butter
2 cups Flour
1 teaspoon Baking Soda
2 Eggs
1 1/2 teaspoons Vanilla
1/3 cup Cocoa
2 cups Sugar
1/2 teaspoon Salt
1/2 cup Buttermilk

    Preheat your oven to 375 degrees. (Topping) Grease and flour a 13" x 9" baking pan. In a medium-sized saucepan, melt the butter over medium heat. Remove from heat and stir in the flour until smooth. Add the brown sugar and eggs and return to the heat. Cook for five minutes, stirring constantly. Remove from the heat, add the vanilla and the pecans, and then set aside. (Brownies) In a saucepan, mix the butter and cocoa together with one cup of water over a low to medium heat, and bring to a boil, stirring constantly. Remove from the heat and set aside. In a mixing bowl, combine the flour, sugar, baking soda, salt, eggs, buttermilk, and vanilla. Add the cocoa mixture and stir until blended and pour into the prepared baking pan. Spoon the topping evenly over the top. Bake for about twenty minutes or until a knife inserted in the center comes out clean. Cool completely and then cut into bars.

Cream Puffs

Cream puffs are a lot easier to make than they sound. Of course, if you try them once, your family will be asking for more.

8 tablespoons Butter   1/8 teaspoon Salt
1 cup Water   1 cup Flour
3 eggs

Heat oven to 450 degrees. Melt the butter in a saucepan and add the salt and water. Bring to a boil. Lower heat to a simmer and add the flour. Stir vigorously until the mixture leaves the sides of the saucepan. Remove from the heat and add and mix one egg at a time. Drop the paste, using a tablespoon onto a greased cookie sheet. Make twelve mounds. Bake for twenty minutes. Reduce the oven heat to 350 degrees and bake another 20 minutes. Place the puffs on a wire rack to cool completely. Cut the puffs in half and fill with whipped cream. Listen to your friends and family ask what bakery that you bought these from.

Mini Eclairs

This is another one of those treats that your friends and family will not believe that you made. I have had the experience of people asking what bakery I bought these from.

Filling
1 package Chocolate Pudding
2 cups Milk
Pastry
8 tablespoons Butter

1/8 teaspoon Salt
4 Eggs
1 cup Water
1 cup Flour

Your favorite Chocolate Fudge Frosting

(**Filling**) Prepare the pudding according to directions and refrigerate for at least one hour. (**Pastry**) Heat oven to 400 degrees. Melt the butter with water and salt until the mixture boils. Stir in the flour all at once until the mixture forms a ball. Pour into a bowl and cool for five minutes. Stir in one egg at a time, mixing after each time you add one. Drop dough into twelve mounds on a well-greased cookie sheet. Using a spoon, pull each mound into a 4" x 1/2" rectangle. Try to round the ends slightly. Bake for thirty-five minutes or until lightly browned. Reduce oven to 375 degrees and bake for ten minutes longer. Cool on a wire rack. With a sharp knife, slice the eclairs in half and spoon in about a tablespoon of the pudding. Replace the top. Spread the tops with the frosting. This will make a dozen eclairs.

Pound Cake

I learned an interesting fact while looking through my recipes for this book. Did you know that the name for this cake came about because it is made with equal weights of butter, sugar, eggs, and flour?

12 tablespoons Butter

3 Eggs

1 teaspoon Baking Powder

1 to 2 tablespoons Milk

3/4 cup Sugar

1 1/2 cup Flour

1 teaspoon Vanilla

Heat oven to 350 degrees. In a mixing bowl, beat the butter until smooth. Add the sugar and beat again until the mixture is light. Add one egg at a time, beating after each addition. Mix in the dry ingredients and vanilla and blend. Add just enough milk to make the mixture drop easily from a spoon. Pour the mixture into a greased 8" springform cake pan or 9" tube pan. (I like to trace the bottom of the pan onto a piece of wax paper. I cut the shape out and place in the bottom of the pan after it has been greased. When the cake is done and cooled, you just slowly peel the paper off and you have a smooth bottomed cake.) Bake for forty-five minutes. When the cake is completely cooled, you can fill or decorate as you wish. I have sprinkled powdered sugar on top, but my favorite is jam. I cut the cake in half through the center and spread it with strawberry jam. Replace the top and cut into wedges.

Madeira Cake

This cake is very much like a pound cake, but it also has a lemon flavor that is a nice complement to a herbal tea.

8 tablespoons Butter
1 1/4 cups Sugar
3 1/4 cups Flour
1 cup Milk

1 teaspoon Lemon Peel
5 Eggs
2 teaspoons Baking Powder

Heat oven to 350 degrees. In a large mixing bowl, cream together the butter and the lemon peel. Add the sugar and beat until light. Mix in one egg at a time with two teaspoons of the flour and blend after each addition. Include the remaining flour and remaining ingredients. Pour the mixture into a greased 8" springform cake pan or 9" tube pan. Bake for sixty minutes. Reduce the oven temperature to 325 degrees and bake another thirty minutes. Cool on a wire rack. Remove from cake pan and cover with powdered sugar.

Gelatin Christmas Cake

I find that my guests really like this dessert after a large Christmas dinner. It is a light dessert that combines the coolness of peppermint and the sweetness of cherries. I serve this with a little bit of peppermint schnapps on the side.

2 tablespoons unflavored Gelatin
2 Eggs, separated
3/4 cup Maraschino Cherries, chopped
4 cups Milk
3/4 cup Sugar
1/3 cup Maraschino Cherry juice
1 dozen Vanilla Wafers
1 1/2 cups Whipped Cream
1/4 teaspoon Peppermint Extract

Soften gelatin in 1/2 cup milk. Scald remaining milk and remove from heat. Add beaten egg yolks, sugar, and softened gelatin. Return to heat and cook until mixture coats spoon. Cool. Add the cherries, cherry juice, and peppermint extract and chill until mixture begins to thicken. Beat the egg whites until stiff peaks form and then add the whipped cream. Fold into gelatin. Butter a gelatin mold and pour in the gelatin mixture. Chill overnight. Unmold and use just a dab of whipped cream to "glue" the vanilla wafers onto the sides and top. Frost the whole thing with whipped cream and sprinkled with green-and-red colored sugars and three or four broken peppermint candies.

Candies

Temperatures and Cold Water
Test for Candy

Temperature (Degrees Fahrenheit)	Stage	Syrup dropped into cold water
234 to 240	Soft Ball	Syrup can be rolled into a soft ball in the water, but goes flat when removed.
250 to 266	Hard Ball	Syrup makes a hard ball in the water, but can still be flattened when removed.
270 to 290	Soft Crack	Syrup separates into strands that bend.
300 to 310	Hard Crack	Syrup separates into strands that are brittle and hard.

Peanut Brittle

2 cups Sugar
2 cups Raw Spanish Peanuts
1 teaspoon Soda

1 cup Light Corn Syrup
1 tablespoon Butter
1/2 teaspoon Salt

Heat the sugar and syrup together with one cup of water in a saucepan until the sugar dissolves. Cook over a medium heat until it reaches a soft ball stage. Add the peanuts and 1/2 teaspoon salt. Cook until the syrup reaches a hard crack stage, stirring often. Remove from heat and quickly stir in the butter and soda. Pour onto a large greased cookie sheet and spread with a spatula. Break into pieces when completely cool.

Anise Candy

1 1/2 cups Sugar
1/4 teaspoon Red Food Coloring

2 cups light Corn Syrup
10 drops oil of Anise

In a saucepan, mix together the sugar, corn syrup and the food coloring and cook until the sugar dissolves. Cook until the syrup reaches a hard crack stage. Remove from heat and stir in the anise oil. Pour onto a greased cookie sheet, spreading with a spatula. Break into pieces when completely cool.

Mexican Coffee Fudge

2 cups Brown Sugar
1 tablespoon Butter

2/3 cup strong Coffee
1 teaspoon Vanilla

Place the brown sugar, coffee, and butter in a saucepan and cook until the candy reaches a soft ball stage. Remove from heat and add the vanilla. Cool to lukewarm without stirring. Beat the mixture until thick and creamy. Add a 1/2 cup nuts if you would like and place in a well buttered pan and refrigerate. Cut into squares.

Baked Caramel Corn

This snack is great for munching while sitting at home watching videos, especially when there are children around. The only problem with this treat is that it doesn't last very long. Real butter is the ingredient in this recipe that makes the taste.

1 cup Butter
2 cups packed Brown Sugar
1/2 cup light Corn Syrup
1 teaspoon Salt

1/2 teaspoon Baking Soda
1 teaspoon Vanilla
6 quarts popped Pop Corn

Preheat oven to 250 degrees. Melt the butter in a sauce pan and then stir in the brown sugar, corn syrup and salt. Bring to a boil without stirring for five minutes. Remove from heat and stir in the baking soda and the vanilla. Place the popped pop corn in a metal roasting pan and pour the caramel mixture over the pop corn mixing well. Bake for one hour, stirring every fifteen minutes. Be very careful because the caramel will be very hot. Remove from oven and cool completely. Break apart and serve.

Desserts

Orange Sherbet

It is a lot easier to make this than it sounds. It just takes a little time. I like to make this for hot summer weekends. It is great to take along on picnics.

1 cup Water   1 1/2 cups Sugar
2 Eggs Whites—stiffly beaten   2 cups Orange Juice
3 tablespoons Lemon Juice

Bring the water and sugar to a boil. Boil for five minutes. While beating the egg whites constantly, pour the syrup in a thin stream into the eggs. Whip in the orange and lemon juice. Pour into a freezer tray and place in the freezer. Stir every half hour. When the sherbet is half frozen, whip again until smooth but not melted. Return to freezer tray and freezer. Freeze overnight. This will make about six servings.

Cantaloupe Sherbet

2 ripe Cantaloupe (3 lbs each)   1/3 cup Sugar
1/3 cup lime Juice   2 tablespoons Honey

Peel the melons, cut in half, and remove the seeds. Cut the melons into small chunks and place in a food processor or blender. Blend just long enough to liquefy. Add the sugar (less if the melons are sweet), lime juice, and honey. Mix well and pour into a bowl that you can use in the freezer. Place in the freezer and stir every half hour for two hours. Place back in the food processor and whip for about ten seconds. Cover with plastic wrap and return to freezer. Freeze for a few hours to harden. Can be served in the center of a wedge of cantaloupe.

Caramel Pecan Cheesecake

If you are tired of the pecan pies for the holidays or find that pecans are very expensive, this is a great recipe. All items here are sold in generic form and a very small bag of pecans is used for this pie. The children seem to love this one.

2 8-oz packages Cream
   Cheese (softened)
1/2 cup Sugar
2 Eggs
1/2 teaspoon Vanilla

20 Caramels
1/2 cup chopped Pecans
2 tablespoons Milk
1 9" Graham Cracker Pie
   Crust

Preheat oven to 350 degrees. Blend together cream cheese, sugar, vanilla, and eggs. Set aside. Melt caramels with milk over a low heat. Add chopped pecans and then spread evenly into pie crust. Pour cream cheese batter over top. Bake for forty minutes or until almost set. Cool and then refrigerate for at least three hours.

Orgasmic Blueberry Pie

I originally named this pie Blueberry-Almond Pie. We had a pot-luck meal one day for lunch where I used to work and we had to draw from a hat to decide what each of us was going to bring in for lunch. I drew dessert. I brought a couple of these pies in to work, and they were a big hit. A friend of mine liked it so much that she said that I should have called it Orgasmic Blueberry Pie and the name stuck.

Blueberry Filling
1 9" Graham Cracker Pie
   Crust
2 tablespoons Cornstarch
2 tablespoons Butter
2 cups Fresh Blueberries
2 tablespoons Sugar
1 tablespoon Lemon Juice
Almond Filling
6 White Chocolate, Almond
   Candy Bars

1 Egg Yolk
1/4 teaspoon Vanilla
1 cup Whipped Cream
2 tablespoons Water
2 tablespoons Powdered
   Sugar
Whipped Cream Layer
1 cup Whipped Cream
1/4 teaspoon Vanilla
1/4 cup Powdered Sugar

(**Blueberry Filling**) Combine cornstarch, sugar, butter, and lemon juice in a saucepan until melted and smooth. Add one cup of the blueberries mashing and stirring until the mixture thickens. Add remaining blueberries and spoon into the pie shell. (**Almond Filling**) Break up the candy bars and melt in a saucepan over low heat. Mix the egg yolk with the water and then stir into the candy bars. Remove from heat and add the vanilla. Mix in the powdered sugar and whipped cream then, spread over the blueberry filling. (**Whipped Cream Layer**) Beat the whipped cream, powdered sugar, and vanilla until stiff peaks form. Spread over the almond filling. Refrigerate overnight.

Cookies and Cream Pie

This is a very nice summer pie. All of the ingredients can be bought in generic or store brand form and taste just as good.

1 Graham Cracker Pie Crust
1 package Vanilla Instant
   Pudding

1 cup crushed Chocolate
   Sandwich Cookies
1 1/2 cups Milk
1 8-oz Whipped Cream

Mix together the milk and instant pudding until well blended. Let stand for at least five minutes. Mix in the whipped cream and cookies and spoon into the graham cracker crust. Freeze for at least five hours. Dip knife in hot water before cutting.

No Bake Apple Pie

I enjoy this pie because it has a sweet-tart flavor that comes from the apples and the grapefruit juice. It also helps that it really does not take a long time to make.

3 medium Apples, sliced
1 9" Graham Cracker Pie
   Crust
3 tablespoons Cornstarch

2 1/2 cups Grapefruit Juice
1/2 cup Sugar
Whipped Cream

Pour the grapefruit juice in a saucepan and heat. Simmer the sliced apples in the juice until tender. Strain the apples from the juice and arrange in the pie shell. Mix the sugar and the cornstarch together and add to the grapefruit juice. Cook and stir until clear and thickened. Pour over the apples and refrigerate for at least three hours. Top with whipped cream before serving.

Apple Custard Pie

6 to 8 Apples—thinly sliced
3/4 cup Sugar
1/2 teaspoon Salt
Cinnamon

1 Pastry Shell
3 tablespoons Flour
1/4 cup Half and Half

Heat the oven to 375 degrees. Place the pastry shell in a greased 9" pie pan. Spread the apple slices into the unbaked pie shell. In a bowl, whisk together the sugar, flour, salt, and cream. Pour the liquid over the apples and sprinkle with cinnamon to taste. Cover the pie loosely with foil. Bake for sixty minutes. Remove the foil and bake for another fifteen minutes or until a knife inserted in the center comes out clean.

Fruit Pizza

I cheat on this one. I do not have a flan pan, so I discovered that I can buy the flan cakes at the store just by themselves. They are very good cakes and I don't tell anyone that I didn't make the cake unless they specifically ask. In today's world you take any compliment that you can get, right?

1 Flan Cake
1 10-oz can Peaches—sliced
1/2 teaspoon Vanilla
1 8-oz Cream Cheese

1/3 cup Sugar
1 tablespoon Cornstarch
Assorted Fruit—(your choice)
    Strawberries, Kiwi, etc.

Beat the cream cheese, sugar, and vanilla until fluffy. Spread over the flan cake. Drain the peaches, but make sure you keep the juice. Show your style by decorating with fruit slices. I start from the outside in with whole strawberries that are all about the same size. Next row in, I place the sliced peaches, then a row of sliced kiwi. I try to get two rows of each, ending with a circle of kiwi in the middle. I then place a small strawberry in the center of the kiwi ring. Pour the peach juice into a measuring cup and add enough water to get one cup liquid. Pour into a saucepan and bring to a boil. Put one tablespoon of water in the measuring cup and add the cornstarch. Stir until smooth and pour into the hot juice. Cook for one minute or until thickened. Spoon over all of the fruit and refrigerate for at least one hour before serving.

Raisin Pie

1 cup Brown Sugar
1 1/2 cups Water
1 teaspoon grated Orange
  Peel
1/3 cup Orange Juice
1/2 cup chopped Walnuts
3 tablespoons Cornstarch

2 cups Raisins
1/2 teaspoon grated Lemon
  Peel
3 tablespoons Lemon Juice
Unbaked Pie Pastry
2 tablespoons Milk

In a saucepan, combine the water and cornstarch until no longer lumpy. Add the sugar, raisins, orange and lemon peel, and the orange and lemon juices. Cook, stirring constantly over a medium heat until the mixture thickens. Stir in nuts and set aside to cool. Preheat oven to 400 degrees. Line a 9" pie plate with an unbaked pastry and add the filling. Place a lattice pastry on top and brush with milk. Sprinkle with sugar and bake for thirty to thirty-five minutes until crust is golden brown.

Cranberry Pie

This pie sounds very tart, but it is actually very good. It is a nice change from the standard pumpkin pies over the holiday season.

4 cups Cranberries
2 tablespoons Flour
3 tablespoons Water
1 1/2 cups Sugar
1/4 teaspoon Salt

1 tablespoon Butter—melted
1 recipe of your favorite Pie
  Pastry—uncooked (See
  Breads for my favorite recipe)

Heat oven to 450 degrees. Chop the cranberries in a food processor and pour into a bowl. Add the remaining ingredients except the pastry and mix well. Line a 9" pie pan with the pastry. Pour in the filling. Arrange pastry in strips on top and bake for fifteen minutes. Reduce oven heat to 350 degrees and bake another thirty minutes.

Layered Pumpkin Pie

This is my family's favorite holiday pie. It has become as traditional as turkey on Thanksgiving. It is a very rich pie and is certainly not for those who are watching the waist line, but then again, that is one of the things that the holiday season is for. Expanding your . . . spirituality.

1 3-oz Cream Cheese, softened
1 tablespoon Half & Half
1 tablespoon Sugar
1 1/2 cups Whipped Cream
1 9" Graham Cracker Pie Crust
2 packages Vanilla Instant Pudding
1 16-oz can Pumpkin
1 teaspoon Cinnamon
1/2 teaspoon Ginger
1/4 teaspoon ground Cloves
1 cup Half & Half

Mix together the cream cheese, one tablespoon half & half, sugar, and whipped cream. Spread into the pie crust. Pour the one cup of half & half into a mixing bowl and add the pudding mix and then beat for one to two minutes. Let stand for about five minutes or until thick. Stir in the pumpkin and spices and mix well. Pour over the cream cheese layer and refrigerate overnight. I garnish each slice with a tablespoon of whipped cream and sprinkle lightly with nutmeg.

Meats

Baked Ham

This is the easiest way that I have found to cook ham so far. Getting up early on holiday mornings to start a meal is really a pain. This recipe saves time and is delicious. You can use the same roasting pan from start to finish, which saves on clean up. Another plus, unless you can get someone else to do the dishes for you.

1 10-pound, boneless Ham
1 Carrot, quartered
6 Peppercorns
1/4 teaspoon Mace
1 1/2 cups Apple Cider

1 Onion, peeled and quar-
   tered
1 Herb Garni (recipe below)
1/4 cup Brown Sugar
1/4 cup Orange Juice

(**Herb Garni**) Cut a 4" square of cheese cloth. In the center, place 3 tablespoons parsley flakes, 1/2 teaspoon thyme, and a bay leaf. Gather the cheese cloth together and close tightly with a bread twist tie. (**Ham**) Place ham in a roasting pan and add enough water to cover. Drop vegetables around the ham and add the peppercorns and Herb Garni. On top of the stove, bring water to boil and then reduce heat. Cover and simmer twenty minutes for each pound. Drain and peel away the skin. Combine the sugar, mace, and orange juice. Place the ham back into the roasting pan and cover with sugar mixture. Pour cider around ham and bake in a 350 degree oven for thirty minutes, basting every ten minutes. Let the ham rest for fifteen minutes before slicing and serving.

Boiled Pork Chops

I know. I thought the same thing. Boiled? Gross. However, this recipe is very good and—God forbid—healthy. I have used the meat spice on different steaks and cooked in the same way. Although very good, it seems to taste the best on pork.

4 Pork Chops   Meat Spice (recipe follows)

Spread two tablespoons of vegetable oil in a large frying pan. Heat the pan to a medium heat. Place the pork chops in the pan and sprinkle with half of the meat spice. Quickly flip the chops and sprinkle with the other half of the spices. Flip the meat again. Chops should be lightly browned on both sides. Drain off the oil and add 1/4 water. Cover and cook for ten minutes, turning the pork chops after five minutes.

Meat Spice

1/4 teaspoon Pepper   1/4 teaspoon Garlic Powder
1/4 teaspoon Onion Powder

Mix completely.

Pork Stuffed Peppers

I really like stuffed green peppers, but it seems like everyone has the same recipe—ground beef, rice, etc. This recipe is very good and is a great change of pace if you like stuffed peppers.

6 Green Peppers
2 tablespoons Butter
3/4 lb ground Ham
2 cups Rice—cooked

4 slices Bacon—cooked and
   crumbled
1 Onion—diced
1/2 teaspoon Paprika
1/2 cup Water

Heat the over to 350 degrees. Cut the stem and top from each pepper and remove the core and seeds. Melt the butter in a frying pan, add the onion and cook until transparent. Add the ham and brown. Drain well. Stir in the paprika and the rice. Fill the peppers with the mixture. Add the water to a cake pan and place the peppers standing upright in the water and cover with foil. Bake for forty minutes. Remove the foil, top each pepper with a slice of uncooked bacon, and bake another ten minutes.

Sausage Rolls

I like this recipe because it can be used for a lot of different times. I have used it for a dinner on the run and for a snack at a New Year's or Super Bowl party.

1 Pie Pastry recipe (see
   Breads)
1 Egg

1 1/2 lbs Ground Sausage
1/2 teaspoon Salt

Heat oven to 400 degrees. Roll the pastry into a rectangle of about 8" wide and 1/8" thick. Cut the dough in half lengthwise. Divide the sausage in half and roll into tube. Place the sausage onto a strip of the dough. Do the same for the other half of the sausage and dough. In a small bowl, beat the egg together with the salt. Brush the edges of the dough with the egg mixture. Roll the dough around the sausage and seal the edges. Brush the whole surface of the dough with the egg mixture. Cut into 3" lengths. Prick each roll with a fork and place on a greased cookie sheet. Refrigerate for fifteen minutes. Bake for fifteen to twenty minutes or until browned. Cool slightly on a wire rack.

Ham and Scalloped Potatoes

6 medium Potatoes
2 slices Bread—crumbled
2 tablespoons Flour
1 teaspoon Salt
1 cup Milk
4 slices Cheese

3 tablespoons Butter
1/2 teaspoon Paprika
1 teaspoon Dry Mustard
1/8 teaspoon Pepper
2 cups Ham—chopped

Peel and slice the potatoes. Boil in salted water for ten to fifteen minutes or until tender. Reserve one cup of the water and drain the remainder off the potatoes. Place the potatoes in a greased two quart casserole dish. Heat oven to 350 degrees. Melt one tablespoon of the butter and mix with the bread crumbs and paprika and set aside. In a saucepan, melt the remaining two tablespoons of butter. Remove from heat and whisk in the flour, dry mustard, salt and pepper. Return to heat and add the milk and reserved potato water. Cook and stir until thickened. Stir in the ham and cheese. Stir until the cheese melts. Pour over the potatoes. Sprinkle with the buttered bread crumbs. Loosely cover with foil and bake for sixty minutes. This will make about six servings.

Beef Soufflé

1 lb Ground Beef
1/2 cup shredded Cheddar
   Cheese
dash of Cayenne Pepper
6 Eggs—divided

1 10-oz can Cream of Mushroom Soup
1/2 teaspoon Marjoram
2 tablespoons Parsley

Heat the oven to 300 degrees. Brown the ground beef in a frying pan and drain completely in a strainer. Heat the soup, cheese, and spices in a saucepan until the cheese melts. Grind the ground beef in a food processor until very fine. Add to the soup mixture. Beat the egg yolks until thick and add to the soup mixture. Beat the egg whites until soft peaks form. Fold the soup mixture into the egg whites and then pour into an lightly greased two-quart casserole dish. Bake for seventy-five minutes and serve immediately. This will make about four servings.

Beef Burritos

1 lb browned Ground Beef
2 teaspoons Onion Powder
1 can Refried Beans
Salsa
Mozzarella Cheese
Flour Tortillas

OPTIONAL
Chopped Lettuce
Sour Cream
Chopped Tomato
Chopped Olives

Flour tortillas usually come in a package of six to eight, so this will serve about three to four people. Heat the refried beans, stirring frequently so that they do not stick. Add the onion powder to the browned ground beef and mix well. Spread about a tablespoon of the refried beans on a flour tortilla up to about a half inch from the edge. Add one or two tablespoons of ground beef on top of the beans. Add cheese and salsa to taste. These are very good as they are. However, you can add any of the optional ingredients to suit your tastes before folding into a burrito.

BBQ Casserole

1 lb Ground Beef
1/2 bottle BBQ Sauce
1 can Refrigerator Biscuits

1/2 medium Onion
4 Slices of Cheese

Heat oven to 350 degrees. Cook the ground beef until browned and add your favorite BBQ sauce. Once heated through, pour into an 8x8x2-inch square pan. Place the cheese slices on top. On top of the cheese, place the biscuits and bake for twenty to twenty-five minutes or until the biscuits are browned.

Taco Pie

1 lb Ground Beef
1 10-oz can Spaghetti Sauce
Grated Parmesan Cheese
8 oz shredded Cheddar
  Cheese
1 8-oz can Refried Beans
1/2 medium Onion—diced

2 tablespoons Taco Seasoning
(See recipe for Taco seasoning)
1 can Croissant Dinner Rolls
Shredded Lettuce—Diced Tomatoes—Sour Cream

Heat oven to 375 degrees. Brown the ground beef and the onion together in a large frying pan and drain. Add the spaghetti
sauce and taco seasoning and simmer for ten minutes. Grease a
10" pie pan. Separate the croissant dough into eight triangles and
place in the pie pan, spreading up the sides of the pan. Sprinkle the
dough with parmesan cheese and bake for five minutes. Spread the
refried beans over the dough, and top with the meat and onion mixture. Sprinkle with the cheddar cheese and bake for fifty to twenty
minutes until the crust is brown. Cut into pie shaped servings and
top with lettuce, tomato, and a dollop of sour cream before serving.

Taco Seasoning

6 teaspoons Chili Powder
2 1/2 teaspoons Garlic Powder
3 teaspoons Onion Powder

4 1/2 teaspoons Cumin
5 teaspoons Paprika
1/8 teaspoon Cayenne Pepper

Combine all ingredients and store in a container with a tight-
fitting lid. This will store up to six months. Makes twenty-one teaspoons, or 1/2 cup. Use two tablespoons for any recipe that calls
for a package of taco seasoning.

Crustless Pizza

This a fast and easy pizza if you do not want to hassle with the dough for the crust. The kids still love it, even though it is a bit unusual.

2 lbs Ground Beef
2 slices of Bread—crumbled
1 Egg
1/8 teaspoon Garlic Powder
1 10-oz can Pizza Sauce
1/4 Onion—chopped
1 teaspoon Salt

1/8 teaspoon Oregano
TOPPINGS—(your choice)
  Sausage, Black Olives,
  Green Pepper, Mushrooms,
  Anchovies, Mozzarella
  Cheese, etc.

Heat the oven to 450 degrees. In a large bowl, mix together the ground beef, 1/2 cup of the pizza sauce, and all other ingredients except for the toppings. Place on a large cookie sheet and press into a 10" circle with a 1" stand-up rim. Bake for ten minutes. Carefully drain off the grease. Spread the rest of the pizza sauce on the pizza and top with your favorite toppings, leaving the mozzarella cheese for last. Bake for ten minutes more. Cut into pizza wedges and serve.

Easy Meatballs

It didn't take long after my divorce until I decided to become creative with my cooking. I mean the one pan hamburger meals can get very boring after a while. There are only so many varieties and so many days of the week. I found this recipe and used it with these hamburger meals to liven them up a bit.

1 Egg	1 slice Bread
2 tablespoons Onion minced	1 tablespoon Parsley
1/8 teaspoon Garlic Powder	1/4 teaspoon Salt
1/8 teaspoon Pepper	1 pound Ground Beef

Crumble the slice of bread into a mixing bowl and then combine all remaining ingredients. Divide the meat mixture into about sixteen equal portions. Make each portion into a meatball and place in a greased 8"x8"x2" microwave safe baking dish in four rows of four. Cover with a sheet of waxed paper. Microwave on high for three minutes. Turn the meatballs, moving the inside meatballs to the outside and the outside meatballs to the inside. Cover and microwave on high for another three minutes. You can use these meatballs for just about any dish. To use these with a one pan hamburger meal, cook the package according to instructions leaving out the hamburger. About ten minutes before the mixture is finished, add the meatballs and cook until heated through.

Baked Meatballs

These meatballs are great with spaghetti. When you are heating the sauce, just add these meatballs and heat through.

1 lb Ground Beef
2 tablespoons Parsley
1/2 medium Onion—diced
1 Egg

1/2 teaspoon Garlic Powder
2 slices of Bread—crumbed
1/2 teaspoon Pepper

Heat oven to 350 degrees. In a large bowl, combine all ingredients and mix well. Form into 1" meatballs. Place on a lightly greased cookie sheet. Bake to thirty minutes.

Meat Loaf

My daughter will not touch any kind of meat loaf. It does not matter how it is prepared. She just looks at it and snubs it off. Therefore, I make this and any other meat loaf for guests when she is not here.

2 lbs Ground Beef
1 cup Milk
1/8 teaspoon Pepper
2 Eggs
1 small Onion—chopped
2 tablespoons Brown Sugar
1/8 teaspoon Ground Nutmeg
2/3 cup Oat Meal

1 teaspoon Salt
1/4 teaspoon Poultry Seasoning
1 teaspoon Worcestershire Sauce
1/4 cup Catsup
1 teaspoon Mustard

Heat oven to 350 degrees. In a large bowl, mix together all the ingredients, except the last four ingredients. Place the meat mixture in a lightly greased 5"x9" loaf pan. Combine in a measuring cup the catsup, brown sugar, mustard, and nutmeg. Mix well. Spread evenly over the meat mixture. Bake for seventy-five minutes. This will serve six to eight people.

Rolled Meat Loaf

This is my favorite meat loaf recipe. The stuffing inside absorbs the juices of the meat and adds a wonderful flavor to the meat.

2 lbs Ground Beef
1/4 teaspoon Pepper
1 1/2 teaspoons Salt
1 Egg
Stuffing
1/2 cup Raisins
1/4 Onion—chopped

1/4 teaspoon Sage
1/4 teaspoon Salt
4 cups Bread—cut into cubes
2 tablespoons Parsley
1/4 teaspoon Pepper
2/3 cup Water with 2 Bouillon Cubes dissolved

Heat oven to 350 degrees. Lightly grease a 5"x9" loaf pan. In a large bowl, mix together the ground beef, salt, pepper, and egg. Spread a sheet of wax paper on your table. Spread the meat mixture on the paper to form a square about 1/2" thick. Mix together the remaining ingredients in the bowl. Spread this mixture over the meat mixture leaving about 1/2" all around the edges. Roll the meat loaf jelly roll style and place in the loaf pan seam side down. Bake for seventy-five minutes. This will make six to eight servings.

Poultry
and
Eggs

Oven Fried Chicken

My daughter and I really like fried chicken, but I for one do not like all of the grease that goes along with it. This is probably the fastest and easiest way to make fried chicken that I have found. Without all the grease.

1 cup Flour   1 package Chicken parts

Preheat oven to 400 degrees. I use a clean plastic grocery bag, and I place the flour in the bag. Flavor the flour with a tablespoon of seasoning salt and maybe 1/2 tablespoon curry powder. It all depends upon what spices you like. Shake each chicken part in the bag and then place on a greased cookie sheet. Bake for thirty minutes and then turn each piece. Bake for another thirty minutes. If you have only small pieces, such as legs and/or wings, change your baking time to twenty-five and twenty-five.

Chicken Nuggets

3 to 4 boneless Chicken   1 Egg
    Breasts   3 1/2 cups Corn-
2 tablespoons Milk   flakes—crushed fine

Heat oven to 400 degrees. Beat egg and milk together in a small mixing bowl. Place the crushed cornflakes into a plastic bag. Cut the chicken breasts into nugget-size pieces. Dip each piece into the egg mixture and then shake in the plastic bag. Place on a greased cookie sheet. Bake for fifteen minutes. Great with warm BBQ sauce for dipping.

One Pan Curry Chicken Dinner

2 tablespoons Cornmeal
4 Chicken Breasts—boneless
1 teaspoon Curry Powder
1/4 cup Butter

4 Carrots—cut into 1" pieces
1 small Onion—cut into rings
4 small Potatoes

Heat the oven to 400 degrees. In a plastic bag, mix the cornmeal and curry powder. Melt the butter in a 9"x13" inch baking pan. Shake the chicken breasts in the plastic bag to coat the chicken. Place in the baking pan. On the other end of the pan, place the carrots, potatoes, and onion. Bake for thirty minutes uncovered. Turn the chicken breasts over and bake another thirty minutes. This recipe will serve four people.

Zippy Chicken & Broccoli

I enjoy spicy foods. However, no one in my family can tolerate them. This recipe is a happy neutral for us. It is an all in one meal, with a zap of spice to wake up our taste buds.

2 tablespoons Butter
4 cups Broccoli
1 small Onion
1 tablespoon Worcestershire
  Sauce
1/2 teaspoon Cayenne Pepper

3 to 4 Chicken
  Breasts—boneless
1 cup Mushrooms
2 Carrots—cut 1" pieces
4 cups cooked Instant Rice

Melt butter in a large frying pan or a wok. Cut the chicken into bite-size pieces and add to the butter, cooking until browned on all sides. Add the broccoli, mushrooms, onion and carrots, and cover. Cook over medium heat until the vegetables are tender. Add the Worcestershire sauce and cayenne pepper and mix with all the ingredients well to make sure chicken and vegetables are completely coated. Serve over cooked rice. This will make four to six servings.

Chicken Alfredo

4 servings Spaghetti
3 to 4 cooked boneless
   Chicken Breasts
1 can Evaporated Milk
2 tablespoons Butter
1/2 medium Onion—diced
1 teaspoon Basil

1 tablespoon Parsley
1/2 cup Parmesan Cheese
1 package Frozen Vegeta-
   bles—(Broccoli, Carrots,
   Cauliflower)
1 teaspoon Oregano
Salt and Pepper to taste

Melt the butter in a large frying pan. Cook the chicken and on-ion until browned on all sides and the onion is transparent. Add the frozen vegetables and simmer until the vegetables are done. Mix the milk, parmesan cheese, and the spices together in a food processor and set aside. Drain the chicken and vegetables and add the milk mixture. Heat through and serve over hot pasta.

Chicken Tetrazzini

On nights when I make spaghetti, I usually always make about two cups extra spaghetti noodles. I place the extra noodles in a plastic container in the refrigerator. In about two or three days, I will make this recipe. Or vice-versa. You just drop the noodles in a strainer and run hot tap water over them to bring them back to life.

3 to 4 boneless Chicken
   Breasts
2 tablespoons Butter
1/2 cup Water
1 tablespoon Parsley

1/4 Onion—chopped
1 10-oz can Cream of Chicken
   Soup
6 slices Cheddar Cheese
2 cups cooked Spaghetti

Melt the butter in a frying pan. Completely cook the chicken that has been cut to bite size pieces together with the onion. Stir in the soup, water, cheese, and parsley. Heat until the cheese melts. Add the spaghetti and cook until heated through. This will make about four servings. (Two, if my daughter is eating.)

Crab Stuffed Chicken Breasts

This is another recipe that your family will think that you slaved hours to prepare for them. I use the bag of pre-cut and cleaned celery and artificial crab meat for this one. The glazed onions are a perfect complement to this dish.

6 boneless Chicken Breasts
1/2 cup chopped Celery
3 tablespoons Dry White Wine (or water)
1 7 1/2-oz package Crab Meat
1/2 cup chopped Onion
3 tablespoons Butter
1/2 cup herb Stuffing Mix
2 tablespoons Flour

1 envelope Hollandaise Sauce Mix
2 tablespoons Dry White Wine (or water)
1/2 cup shredded Swiss Cheese
1/2 teaspoon Paprika
3/4 cup Milk
2 tablespoons melted Butter

Preheat oven to 375 degrees. Pound chicken breasts to 1/4" thick and sprinkle with salt and pepper. Cook onion and celery in the butter until tender. Remove from heat and add the wine, crab meat, and stuffing mix. Mix well. Place about 1/2 cup stuffing on the breasts. Roll up and secure each with a toothpick. Combine the flour and paprika and coat each chicken breast. Place the breasts in a 8"x8"x2" baking dish and drizzle with two tablespoons of melted butter. Bake uncovered for one hour. Arrange the chicken breasts in a circle pattern on your serving platter. Heat the hollandaise sauce mix and milk until thick. Add wine and cheese. Stir until cheese melts. Spoon over each chicken breast and serve. I like to garnish the platter with lemon slices in the center and a parsley sprig in the center of the lemons.

Pepperoni Stuffed Chicken Breasts

I don't make this recipe too often. It is very rich and a little expensive to make. The ingredients are difficult to find generic substitutes for. However the finished product is well worth the effort.

6 boneless Chicken Breasts
1/2 cup chopped Pepperoni
2 teaspoons minced Shallots
3 Eggs

1/2 cup Fonitina Cheese
1 cup chopped Broccoli
4 tablespoons Butter
1 cup dry Bread Crumbs

Pound chicken breasts to 1/4" thick and salt and pepper lightly. Melt three tablespoons butter and sauté broccoli for three minutes. Add the pepperoni and remove from heat. Add the shallots and cheese and let cool. Place about 1/2 cup of the stuffing mix on each chicken breast, roll up and secure with toothpicks. Refrigerate for three to four hours. Preheat oven for 350 degrees. Beat the eggs, dip each breast in the egg, and then in the dry bread crumbs. Brown each breast, seam side down first, in a frying pan of one tablespoon of melted butter. Brown on all sides. Place the breasts in a casserole dish and bake for fifteen minutes.

Sauce
1/2 cup Gorgonzola Cheese
2 tablespoons minced Shallots

1 1/2 cups Whipping Cream,
   unwhipped
Parmesan cheese

In a saucepan, bring the whipping cream to a simmer. Add the shallots and simmer for four minutes. Stir in the gorgonzola cheese until it melts. Add just enough parmesan cheese to thicken. Pour sauce on your serving platter. Slice the chicken breasts from the center out to one side in several slices. Fan the breasts out on top of the sauce. I usually serve this with some hot glazed carrots.

Beer Batter for Chicken

2 Eggs
2/3 cup Beer
1 cup Flour

2 tablespoons Oil
1/2 teaspoon Salt

Combine all ingredients together. Dip the chicken into the batter and fry in oil (enough oil to deep fry), heated to 375 degrees. This will take about fifteen to twenty minutes or until golden brown. Drain on paper towels.

Chicken Balls

No. This recipe has nothing to do with the chicken's anatomy.

1/2 Onion
1 tablespoon Sugar
1 tablespoon Soy Sauce
Frying Oil

3 to 4 boneless Chicken
   Breasts—boiled
1/2 tablespoon Water
1 Egg

Heat the frying oil. In a food processor, grind very fine the onion and the chicken. Pour into a bowl and add the remaining ingredients. Roll into 1" diameter meatballs. Deep fry until brown on all sides. Serve with French fries.

Roast Turkey

Our family usually always has turkey for Thanksgiving. One year I volunteered to cook for the family on Thanksgiving, having never roasted a turkey before in my life. Seeing I was extremely nervous, a friend of mine gave me this easy cooking chart and it was so simple. The turkey came out golden brown and juicy.

Weight (lbs)	Unstuffed (hours)	Weight (lbs)	Stuffed (hours)
8–12	2 3/4–3	8–12	3–3 1/2
12–14	3–3 3/4	12–14	3 1/2–4
14–18	3 3/4–4 1/4	14–18	4–4 1/4
18–20	4 1/4–4 1/2	18–20	4 1/4–4 3/4
20–24	4 1/2–5	20–24	4 3/4–5 1/4

Bring four cups of water to a boil with six chicken bouillon cubes. Boil until dissolved. Pour broth into roasting pan and then place completely thawed turkey in it. Cover leg ends and wing tips with foil. Roast turkey in a preheated, 350 degree oven, basting every thirty minutes. Use a meat temperature gauge to check for doneness. Turkey is done when the temperature in the thigh reaches at least 180 degrees and the thickest part of the breast reaches at least 170 degrees. Let the turkey rest for fifteen minutes before carving.

Orange Stuffing (per 5 pounds)

2 cups finely diced Celery
3 cups toasted Bread Crumbs
2/3 cup diced Orange sec-
tions
1/2 teaspoon Poultry Seasoning

1/4 cup Butter, melted
1 teaspoon Orange Peel,
grated
1/2 teaspoon Salt
1 Egg, beaten

Cook celery in the butter until tender, but not brown. Add re-maining ingredients and a dash of black pepper and toss lightly. Stuff the turkey after removing the bag containing the neck and giblets.

Scalloped Eggs

4 1/2 tablespoons Butter
1 cup Milk
1/2 teaspoon Worcestershire
Sauce
6 Eggs—hard boiled

1 1/2 tablespoons Flour
1/4 teaspoon Salt
2 slices Bread—crumbled
1/2 cup shredded Cheddar
Cheese

Melt 1 1/2 tablespoons of the butter in a saucepan. Remove from heat and whisk in the flour and milk. Season with salt and a dash of pepper and return to heat. Stir over heat until thickened and then set aside. Heat the oven to 350 degrees. Melt the remain-ing three tablespoons of butter and add 1/4 cup of the crumbled bread and set aside. In a lightly greased casserole dish, place the remaining bread crumbs, then slice the eggs and place them on top next. Put the cheese on top of the eggs and then the Worcestershire sauce. Top with the buttered bread crumbs. Bake for thirty min-utes or until the top is slightly browned. This will make four to six servings.

Egg and Sausage Casserole

1 lb Cooked Breakfast Sausage
1/4 cup Butter
2 cups Milk

2 Slices of Bread
4 Eggs—hard boiled
4 tablespoons Flour
1 can Whole Corn

Heat oven to 375 degrees. Slice two of the hard boiled eggs and place the slices in a greased 1 1/2 casserole dish. Melt the butter in a sauce pan and stir in the flour to make a paste. Add the milk and heat until thickened. Stir in the corn and the sausage. Pour the mixture on top of the sliced eggs. Slice the other two eggs and place on top. Crumb the slices of bread on top and bake for thirty minutes.

Cheese and Bacon Quiche

This is a great recipe to prepare for guests with a green salad on the side.

Crust
1 1/3 cups Flour
8 teaspoons Butter
1/8 teaspoon Salt
2 to 3 tablespoons Water
Filling
10 slices Bacon—cooked and crumbled

4 Eggs
1/4 teaspoon Thyme
1/2 cup shredded Cheddar Cheese
1 1/2 cups Milk
1/8 teaspoon Pepper
1/2 cup shredded White Cheddar Cheese

(**Crust**) Mix the flour and the salt together in a mixing bowl. Cut in the butter until crumbs form. Add water one tablespoon at a time until a dough forms. Shape into a disk and wrap in plastic wrap. Refrigerate for thirty minutes. Heat oven to 375 degrees. Roll the dough out on a lightly floured surface to make a 11" circle. Place in a 9" pie pan and trim the edge. Prick the dough with a fork and bake for twelve minutes or until <u>lightly</u> browned. Cool pan on a wire rack. (**Filling**) Whisk together the eggs, milk, thyme, and pepper. Pour into the crust. Sprinkle the egg mixture with the crumbled bacon. Mix together the cheeses and sprinkle on top of bacon. Bake about thirty minutes or until custard is set. Serve warm.

Spanish Scrambled Eggs

6 Eggs
2 tablespoons Butter
Salsa
1 tablespoon Parsley
1/4 cup Milk

1/4 cup Onion—diced
2 tablespoons Green Pep-
  per—diced
2 tablespoons Tomato—diced

Beat together the eggs, milk, parsley, and just enough pepper to taste and set aside. Melt the butter in a large frying pan. Sauté the onions until limp. Add the green peppers and tomatoes and cook until heated through. Mix in the eggs and stir continuously until the eggs are cooked through. Scoop onto plates with toast and top with salsa just before serving.

Demon Eggs

I had a bit of difficulty trying to decide where to place this recipe. I was going to place it up with the appetizers, but I decided to place it with the egg recipes. In any case, I have found that these eggs do not last long enough to care where they are placed. I have had friends and relatives tell me that they have never had anything other than the standard deviled eggs. This recipe will make thirty-six deviled egg halves.

18 Eggs—hard boiled
1 cup Mushrooms
8 tablespoons Butter
1 can cooked Chicken
1 can Tuna
1 8-oz Cream Cheese
Sauce

3 tablespoons Butter
2 cups Milk
3 tablespoons Flour
Garnish
1 can Pimientos
Pickles
1 can Black Olive halves

Slice all of the eggs in half lengthwise and remove the yolks. Press the yolks through a fine sieve. Mix the yolks with seven tablespoons of the butter. Keep the egg whites in a bowl of cold water. Cook the mushrooms in the last tablespoon of butter. Drain the can of chicken and pour into a food processor. Add the mushrooms and grind very fine. Pour into a bowl. (**Sauce**) Melt the butter in a saucepan. Remove from heat and whisk in the flour and milk. Return to heat, stir and cook until thickened. Cool. Divide the egg yolk and butter mixture into three parts, one part in with the chicken mixture, the second part into the well-drained tuna, and the third part into the softened cream cheese. Add just enough sauce to the mixtures to bind them together, but do not make too thin. Refrigerate everything until about an hour before serving. Before serving, use a pastry bag and pipe chicken mixture into twelve egg halves. Rinse the bag thoroughly and repeat for the tuna mixture. Repeat for the cheese mixture. The different garnishes are basically used to identify which is which. A piece of pimiento on top of the chicken, an olive on top of the tuna, and a pickle on top of the cream cheese. Of course, you can use whatever you would like for garnish. Place eggs on a serving platter and enjoy.

Vegetables

Baked Sweet Potatoes

I could never get my daughter to eat sweet potatoes. Potatoes of any kind, as far as that goes. She will eat these, however. It is probably just because of the marshmallows.

1 pound can Sweet Potatoes   1/2 cup Mini Marshmallows
3/4 cup packed Brown Sugar   1 teaspoon Salt
1/4 cup Butter

Grease 1 1/2 quart casserole dish and preheat oven to 375 degrees. Combine brown sugar and salt. Layer in the casserole dish the potatoes and sugar mixture ending with the sugar mixture. Bake for twenty-five minutes. Remove from oven, add the mini marshmallows, and bake another five minutes.

Sweet-Potato Casserole

I love this recipe as a different type of vegetable dish to serve. It is made with regular potatoes, but it has a sweetened taste to it. Very nice for pot luck dinners.

4 to 5 medium Potatoes   1/4 cup Butter
1/2 teaspoon Salt   1/8 teaspoon Pepper
1/3 cup Milk   1 cup shredded Cheddar
1/2 cup Whipped Cream   Cheese

Peel and boil the potatoes until tender. Heat oven to 350 degrees. Drain. In a large mixing bowl, mash the potatoes together with the butter, seasonings, and milk. Pour into a lightly greased two-quart casserole dish. Mix together the cheese and the whipped cream and scoop on top of the potatoes. Bake for twenty-five minutes or until browned. This will make about four to six servings.

Naked Baked Potatoes

These potatoes make a very attractive dish when served with steak or chops. Definitely use real butter for these.

4 medium Potatoes
3 tablespoons Butter
1 teaspoon Cumin
1/2 cup shredded Cheddar
  Cheese

1 teaspoon Salt
1 tablespoon each—Parsley,
  Chives, Thyme
1/4 cup Parmesan Cheese

Heat oven to 425 degrees. Peel the potatoes and rinse in cold water. Place a spoon handle on the side of the potato and cut the potato into thin slices, using the spoon handle so as not to cut all the way through. Place the potatoes into a baking dish and fan slightly. Mix the parsley, chives, thyme, and cumin together in a small bowl. Sprinkle the spices over the potatoes. Melt the butter and drizzle over the top of the potatoes. Bake for fifty minutes. Sprinkle with the cheeses that have been mixed together and bake for another ten to fifteen minutes until lightly browned and potatoes are soft inside.

Baked French Fries

2 medium Potatoes

1/2 teaspoon Salt

Heat oven to 425 degrees. Lightly grease a cookie sheet. Peel the potatoes and cut into 1/4" strips. Place the potatoes in a single, flat layer on the cookie sheet. Sprinkle with the salt and bake for twenty-five minutes or until browned.

Baked Vegetables

This recipe goes really well with steak or pork chops. Add a little French bread with garlic butter and you have a complete meal.

1 small bag Baby Carrots
2 jars Baby Onions, drained
2 cans whole Potatoes,
   drained
1 small Green Pepper

1 small Red Pepper
1/8 teaspoon Pepper
2 tablespoons Butter
3/4 teaspoon Salt
1 recipe medium White Sauce

Preheat oven to 350 degrees. Place drained onions and potatoes with the carrots in a greased two-quart baking dish. Cut both peppers into strips and arrange on top. Season with salt and pepper. Make your white sauce (see Soup and Sauce section) and then pour over the top, covering all vegetables. Slice your butter into small patties and arrange on top. Bake for 1 1/2 hours or until vegetables are done completely through.

Broccoli Parmesan

I made this recipe for our latest Christmas dinner, just to have something different for a vegetable choice. It was a big hit with the family members. Even from those who would not ordinarily eat broccoli.

2 10-oz frozen Broccoli Spears
2 tablespoons Butter
2/3 cup Milk
1/4 Onion—chopped

1 10-oz can Cream of Chicken
   Soup
1/3 cup Parmesan Cheese

Cook the broccoli in water until tender. Drain well. Melt the butter in a saucepan and cook the onion until transparent. Pour the soup, milk, and cheese in with the onions. Cook until heated through. Place the broccoli spears on your serving plate and pour the sauce over the top and serve.

Glazed Onions

This is a nice recipe to serve alongside a poultry dish. My friends and family love this side dish, but I have yet to give them the recipe. It is very easy to prepare, yet tastes like it took hours to make. Some things are better left unsaid.

2 jars Baby Whole Onions   4 tablespoons Butter
2 tablespoons Sugar

Drain the onions, reserving 1/2 cup of the liquid. In a skillet, combine the liquid, sugar, and butter. Cook until blended. Add the onions and cook for ten minutes or until lightly browned, stirring often.

Candied Carrots

1/3 cup Brown Sugar   8 Carrots—cooked until
                             tender
                          2 tablespoons Butter

Melt the butter in frying pan. Mix in the brown sugar and stir until the sugar is melted. Add the cooked carrots and simmer for about ten minutes, stirring occasionally to keep from sticking.

Mashed Carrots

1 lb Carrots—cooked until   1/8 teaspoon Pepper
   tender   1/4 cup Milk
3 tablespoons Butter

Mash the hot cooked carrots and add the pepper, butter, and milk. Mix well. Heat again in the microwave if necessary.

Creamed Peas and New Potatoes

1 1/2 pounds (about 15) tiny New Potatoes. (You can use large potatoes. Cut into quarters if you cannot find New Potatoes.)
1 can Peas

4 tablespoons Butter
2 cups Milk
3 tablespoons Green Onion
4 tablespoons Flour
1 recipe medium White Sauce

Scrub new potatoes to remove dirt and then peel a single strip around the center. Cook in boiling water for about fifteen to twenty minutes and drain. Meanwhile, cook the can of peas in their juice with the onion for eight to ten minutes and then drain. Make the white sauce. Put the potatoes and peas into a serving bowl and then pour the white sauce over the top. Garnish with parsley flakes.

Tangy Green Beans

This recipe has a tart flavor because of the mustard and Worcestershire sauce. Surely not for the weak palate.

2 slices Bacon, cooked, crumbled
1 teaspoon Dijon Mustard
1 9-oz package frozen Green Beans

2 tablespoons Bacon grease
1/4 teaspoon Tabasco Sauce
1 teaspoon Worcestershire Sauce

In a small bowl, combine the bacon grease, mustard, Worcestershire sauce, and Tabasco sauce. Set aside. Cook beans in a covered microwave-safe bowl, in the microwave on high for 3 1/2 minutes. Stir and cook another 3 1/2 minutes. Drain and then pour beans back into the microwave bowl. Pour the mustard mixture over the top and mix well. Cook in the microwave on high for one minute. Crumble the bacon over the top and serve.

Salads

Vinegarette Salad Dressing

This recipe is a very nice change to the standard vinegar and oil dressing. I created this recipe when trying to combine two recipes for salad dressings because I didn't have the complete ingredients for either one. A regular vinegar can be used instead of the red wine vinegar. I started the recipe using just the white vinegar. However, I have found that the red wine vinegar adds a crisp taste to the dressing.

1/4 cup Red Wine Vinegar
1/2 teaspoon Salt
dash Paprika
2 tablespoons Parsley

1/2 Salad or Vegetable Oil
1/4 teaspoon Pepper
2 teaspoons Worcestershire
  Sauce

Combine all ingredients in a dressing server and shake well. Shake again just before pouring over your favorite green salad. I have found that in your local grocery you can buy mixed greens which are different types of lettuce greens. I use these greens topped with sliced radish, onion, hard boiled egg, carrot and bean sprouts. Then top with the dressing and a few croutons.

Raspberry Walnut Dressing

1 cup fresh Raspberries
2 tablespoons Vinegar

1/2 cup Apple Juice Concentrate
1/3 cup Walnuts—chopped

In a blender, blend the raspberries, concentrate, and vinegar together until smooth. Pour through a fine strainer to remove the seeds. Add the chopped walnuts and pour into your favorite dressing server.

Thai Chicken Salad

Do not let the ingredients in this recipe stop you from trying it. It is a little strange, but it is simply delicious. This recipe will serve four people.

1 head of Lettuce
1/2 package Frozen Vegetables (Broccoli, Carrots, Cauliflower)
4 tablespoons Vegetable Oil
2 tablespoons Soy Sauce
1/4 teaspoon Red Pepper (Cayenne)

3 to 4 boneless Chicken Breasts
2 tablespoons Red Wine Vinegar
2 tablespoons smooth Peanut Butter
1/4 teaspoon Garlic Powder

Shred the lettuce and place into a large serving bowl. Heat two tablespoons of oil in a frying pan and cook the chicken that has been cut into bite size pieces. Add the frozen vegetables and simmer until the vegetables are done and tender. In a bowl, mix this dressing with a blender until smooth—vegetable oil, vinegar, soy sauce, peanut butter, cayenne pepper, and garlic powder. When the chicken and vegetables are done, toss the lettuce with the dressing to coat completely. Place the chicken and vegetable mixture on top and serve.

Taco Salad

4 Flour Tortillas
1 teaspoon Chili Powder

2 tablespoons Oil

Microwave the tortillas for forty-five seconds or until softened. Mix together the oil and chili powder in a small bowl. Brush the oil mixture on both sides of the tortillas. Place the tortillas in soup bowls, folding inward to fit. Microwave for 2 1/2 minutes, turn and microwave for 2 1/2 minutes longer. Remove from bowls and cool on a wire rack. **Bowls will be very hot.**

1 lb Ground Beef
3/4 cup Water
1 Green Pepper—chopped
2 tablespoons Taco Seasoning
1 head of Lettuce

1/2 cup sliced Black Olives
8 oz shredded Cheddar
  Cheese
Salsa—Sour Cream

Shred the lettuce and divide into the taco bowls. Fill only 3/4 full. In a frying pan, brown the ground beef. Add the taco seasoning and water and simmer for ten minutes, stirring occasionally. Place the green pepper and olives on the lettuce and top with one or two scoops of the meat mixture. Sprinkle with the cheddar cheese, add a dollop of sour cream, and top the sour cream with a bit of salsa.

Homemade Mayonnaise

This mayonnaise is made in a blender, is quick and easy, and is less expensive than buying it at the store.

1 Egg
2 tablespoons Lemon Juice
1 teaspoon Dijon Mustard

1 cup Salad or Olive Oil
dash Tabasco Sauce
1/2 teaspoon Salt

Place 1/4 cup of the oil in a blender with the rest of the ingredients. Blend on high speed until smooth. Add the remainder of the oil and blend until thick and smooth.

Sour Cream Salad Dressing

1 teaspoon Salt
1/8 teaspoon Cayenne Pepper
2 tablespoons Vinegar
1 tablespoon Sugar

1 tablespoon Lemon Juice
1 cup Sour Cream with
   Chives

Combine all ingredients together and mix well.

Sour Cream Potato Salad

Personally, I do not like mayonnaise. I am always trying to find an alternative to it. This is a potato salad that I took along to a Fourth of July party, and it was a big hit.

4 cups sliced, cooked Potatoes
1 medium, minced Onion
1 1/2 teaspoons Salt
3 hard boiled Eggs
1/4 cup Vinegar

1/2 cup diced Cucumber
3/4 teaspoon Celery Seed
1/2 teaspoon Pepper
2 cups Sour Cream and
   Chives
1 teaspoon prepared Mustard

Lightly toss together the potatoes, cucumber, onion, celery seed, salt and pepper. Separate the egg yolks from the egg whites. Dice the egg whites and add to the potato mixture. Break apart the egg yolks in a sauce pan, then add the sour cream, vinegar, and mustard. Heat just until warm and pour over the potatoes and toss lightly. Refrigerate until needed, but do not make too far in advance. The potatoes will get a little pasty if in the refrigerator for too long.

Improvised Crab Louis

I use artificial crab meat for this recipe. However, I understand that a few people are allergic. You might want to check with your guests before using the artificial crab meat. This makes a nice lunch on a hot summer day, with a glass of herbal ice tea on the side.

3 cups chopped Crab Meat
2 hard boiled Eggs diced
1/4 cup Whipped Cream
1/4 cup chopped Onion
1/4 cup Salsa

2 large Tomatoes diced
1 cup Mayonnaise
1/4 cup chopped Green Pepper
1 teaspoon Lemon Juice

Mix together the mayonnaise, whipped cream, green pepper, onion, lemon juice, and the salsa. Lightly toss in the crab meat, tomatoes, and the diced eggs. Chill for about an hour before serving. I recommend a Chinese lettuce leaf on a saucer and using an ice-cream scoop to place the salad on the lettuce. Garnish with a twisted lemon wedge on the top center of the salad.

Rice and Ham Salad

This is a tangy salad that goes well with a ham dinner. I highly recommend that you not use a quick cook or ready cooked rice for this one. The salad becomes too thick, like paste. When reading the ingredients, it does seem like a lot of vegetables. However, if you keep in mind the small bags of already cut and cleaned vegetables I previously mentioned, this recipe is fairly inexpensive. The French dressing and the mayonnaise can be bought in very small containers if you are like me and don't keep it around the house anyway.

1 1/3 cups cooked Long Grain Rice
3/4 cup Mayonnaise
1 teaspoon Curry Powder
1/2 teaspoon Prepared Mustard
1 15-oz can Peas, drained
1/2 cup sliced Radishes

1/4 cup French Salad Dressing
1 tablespoon chopped Green Onion
1/2 teaspoon Salt
1 cup sliced Raw Cauliflower
1/2 cup chopped Celery
1 8-oz package square, sandwich sliced, cooked ham

Keep all the ham slices piled on top of each other and slice thin strips from one side to the other. Combine the cooked rice and French dressing and chill for several hours. Just before serving, mix the remaining ingredients. I recommend placing a red-veined leaf lettuce on a saucer and then use an ice-cream scoop to place the salad in the center of the lettuce leaf. Sprinkle lightly with paprika.

Cinnamon—Apple Salad

This is a wonderful Christmastime salad. The red hot candies can be found in the cake decorating area of your grocery store and add the special flavor to this jello salad. For an extra festive touch, I like to add a few drops of green food coloring to the cream-cheese mixture before placing it on top of the salad.

2 3-oz packages Lemon Jello
2 cups Applesauce
2 3-oz packages Cream
  Cheese
2 tablespoons Mayonnaise

1/2 cup Red Cinnamon Candies
1 tablespoon Lemon Juice
1/4 cup Milk

Combine jello and cinnamon candies in three cups of hot water and stir until dissolved. Stir in the applesauce and the lemon juice. Pour into a 8"x8"x2" pan and chill until partially set. Mix together the cream cheese, milk, and mayonnaise and spoon onto the jello in different locations. Use a butter knife and swirl through the jello. Do not mix together. Chill until completely set.

Sunshine Salad

1 lb Carrots
1/2 cup Raisins

1 8-oz Vanilla Yogurt

Use a potato peeler and peel off the skins of the carrots. Then use the peeler to peel the remainder of the carrot in a bowl. Repeat for the remaining carrots. Stir in the yogurt and raisins. Refrigerate for at least thirty minutes. Serve on lettuce leaves. This will make about four to six servings.

Soups, Sauces,
Sandwiches,
and Gravy

Gazpacho

This is a tomato soup that is meant to be served cold. Of course when I first heard of it, it took me a while to try it. Old fashioned as I am, I thought that soups were meant to be served hot and I just couldn't imagine a cold soup. Since then, I have found a few cold soups that I really like. I hope you enjoy.

2 cups hot Water
20 oz can of Tomato Juice
2 tablespoons minced Onion
1/4 teaspoon Tabasco Sauce
dash Pepper
1 cup chopped Cucumber

4 Beef Bouillon cubes
3 tablespoons Lemon Juice
1/8 teaspoon Garlic Powder
1/2 teaspoon Salt
1 cup chopped Green Pepper
1 cup chopped Tomato

Place the bouillon cubes in the hot water and microwave on high for five minutes. Pour into a large bowl that will fit into your freezer. Add the tomato juice, lemon juice, onion, garlic powder, Tabasco sauce, salt and pepper. Chill in your refrigerator for four hours. Meanwhile, chop the green pepper, cucumber, and tomato and place in a bowl with a lid also in the refrigerator. Place the soup mixture in your freezer one hour before you are ready to serve. When you are ready to serve, place a couple of spoons of the chopped vegetable mixture into your soup dishes and pour the soup over the top. Garnish with a bit of chopped basil and croutons.

Cucumber Soup

2 medium Cucumbers
1 tablespoon chopped Green
  Onion

1 teaspoon Salt
1 quart Buttermilk
1/4 cup chopped Parsley

Peel the cucumbers and chop very fine. Add the remainder of the ingredients and mix well. Cover and chill for at least four hours. Stir before serving. I like to garnish this one with a thin slice of cucumber floating in the center and a sprig of parsley on the edge of the soup bowl.

Texas Chili

This is a basic recipe for a very good chili. Make it with or without beans and as spicy as you would like. I had to find a neutral recipe because I like spicy foods and my daughter does not. I found that one tablespoon of the chili powder is just about right. The cumin seed is the spice that adds the flavor to the chili and is the "secret ingredient" in taco seasoning.

1 1/2 pounds Ground Beef
1/4 teaspoon Garlic Powder
1 6-oz can Tomato Paste
1 15-oz can Red Kidney
   Beans

Salt and Pepper to taste
1 large chopped Onion
1 8-oz can Tomato Sauce
1 teaspoon Cumin Seed
1 tablespoon Chili Powder

Brown the ground beef in a stew pot. Do not drain off the fat. Add chopped onion and garlic powder and cook together for five minutes. Stir in the tomato sauce and its can full of water, the tomato paste and its can full of water, the kidney beans and its can full of water and then add the cumin seed. Simmer covered on the stove for at least two hours, stirring occasionally. Add water as needed to make as thin or as thick as you would like. One hour before serving, add the chili powder and salt and pepper to taste. Tastes great on a cold evening with a grilled cheese sandwich.

Hearty Chili

This is my personal favorite of all chili recipes. Of course my daughter does not like it because of all of the vegetables, but oh, well. I make it when she spends the night somewhere else.

1 lb Ground Beef
1 small Green Pepper—diced
1 8-oz can Chili Beans
1 16-oz can V8 Juice
1 tablespoon Chili Powder
Shredded Cheddar Cheese

1 medium Onion—diced
2 Celery stalks—chopped
2 cans Tomato Paste
1 tablespoon Worcestershire
   Sauce
1/8 teaspoon Garlic Powder

In a stew pan, cook the ground beef, onion, green pepper, and celery about ten minutes or until the ground beef is browned. Add the beans with their liquid and all of the remaining ingredients except the cheddar cheese. Bring to a boil. Reduce heat and simmer for about ten minutes longer. Serve in soup bowls and garnish with the shredded cheese.

Hamburger Soup

Served with a warm wheat bread, this is a whole meal in one.

2 pounds Ground Beef
1/4 teaspoon Pepper
1/4 teaspoon Basil
1 package Onion Soup Mix
1 8-oz can Tomato Sauce
1 cup chopped Celery
1 cup sliced Carrots
Grated Parmesan Cheese

1/2 teaspoon Salt
1/4 teaspoon Oregano
1/4 teaspoon Seasoning Salt
6 cups Water
1 tablespoon Soy Sauce
1/4 cup Celery Leaves
1 cup uncooked Elbow Macaroni

Brown the ground beef in a stew pot and do not drain. Add the salt, pepper, oregano, basil, seasoning salt, and onion soup mix. Stir together with the water, tomato sauce, and soy sauce. Bring to boiling then cover and simmer for fifteen minutes. Add the chopped celery, celery leaves, and carrots. Simmer for thirty minutes. Stir in the macaroni and simmer thirty minutes longer, stirring occasionally. Add more water if necessary. Scoop into serving bowls and sprinkle with grated parmesan cheese before serving.

Meatball and Vegetable Soup

This is my favorite recipe. It was the first recipe that I created myself. I was looking to make a soup of some kind with hamburger and couldn't find one among my recipes. I then combined three recipes and came up with this one. My daughter really likes it and I hope you do too.

6 cups Water
4 medium chopped Carrots
1 medium chopped Onion
6 Beef Bouillon cubes

3 chopped Celery stalks with leaves
8 whole, peeled Baby Potatoes

(Sometimes if I cannot find the baby potatoes, I use a bag of frozen stew vegetables instead of the carrots, celery, onion, and potatoes.)

1 pound Ground Beef
1/2 cup Oatmeal
1/2 teaspoon Salt
1/2 teaspoon Parsley

1 Egg
1/8 teaspoon Garlic Powder
1/8 teaspoon Oregano
1/2 cup Parmesan Cheese

Bring the water and the bouillon cubes to a boil. Stir until the bouillon cubes are dissolved. Add the vegetables and bring back to a boil. Reduce heat and simmer until the vegetables are nearly done. Meanwhile, mix together the ground beef, egg, oatmeal, garlic powder, salt, oregano and parsley. Roll meatballs into sizes about one inch diameter and drop into the soup. Simmer for fifteen minutes and then add the parmesan cheese. Simmer for another thirty minutes, stirring occasionally and then serve.

Pumpkin Soup

This is a great soup served before an elegant Thanksgiving meal. Garnish with a small sprig of rosemary in the center of the bowl of soup.

1 pound can of pumpkin
1/2 pound chopped Carrots
4 cups Water
Pinch of Sugar
3 tablespoons Whipped
   Cream

2 teaspoons Basil
1/2 pound canned tomatoes
Salt and Pepper to taste
6 Chicken Bouillon cubes
1 medium chopped Onion
1/4 cup Butter

Bring water and bouillon cubes to a boil in a stew pot. Put in the carrots and cook until tender. Sauté the onion in a small saucepan with the butter. Mix all of the remaining ingredients and onions very thoroughly in the stew pot. Pour into a large bowl. Fill a blender half full with the contents of the bowl and puree until smooth. Pour back into stew pot. Repeat for the remainder of the contents of the bowl. Heat the soup in the stew pot until warm all the way through and then serve.

Beef Stew

Winters in South Dakota can be very cold and difficult to get around. This stew is fast, easy, and with some biscuits on the side, is a complete meal. It does a great job of warming you up on a cold winter night too. I usually find the stew meat in the grocery store for less than two dollars. I have used stir-fry beef and the flavor is still very good.

2 lbs Stew Meat
2 cups Water
2 tablespoons Butter
4 Beef Bouillon Cubes
1 teaspoon Worcestershire
  Sauce
1 Onion—diced
1/4 teaspoon Pepper

6 Carrots—cut to 1" pieces
1/3 cup Water
1/8 teaspoon Garlic Powder
1 teaspoon Sugar
dash of Cloves
4 Potatoes—quartered
3 tablespoons Flour

In a large pan, melt the two tablespoons of butter and brown the stew meat, turning often. Melt the bouillon cubes in the two cups of water. Stir the water, Worcestershire sauce, garlic powder, onion, sugar, pepper, and cloves in with the meat. Cover and simmer for 1 1/2 hours, stirring occasionally to keep from sticking. Add the carrots and potatoes and simmer for an additional thirty minutes or until the vegetables are tender. In a measuring cup, measure the 1/3 cup water and stir in the flour until completely smooth. Pour into the hot stew stirring constantly and cook until thickened. This will make four to six servings.

Savory Beef Stew

This is my family's favorite stew. It is good for any season of the year and with its slightly sweet flavor, even the children like it.

2 lbs Stew Meat
1/2 cup Catsup
4 tablespoons Red Wine Vinegar
1 cup Water
2 Carrots—cut into 1-inch pieces

4 tablespoons Butter
4 tablespoons Brown Sugar
3 teaspoon Worcestershire Sauce
1 10-oz jar Pearl Onions
Chopped Parsley

Melt the butter in a large stew pan. Brown the meat on all sides in the butter. Add the catsup, brown sugar, vinegar, Worcestershire sauce, water, and onions. Cover and simmer for one hour and fifteen minutes. Stir occasionally. Add the carrots and simmer for forty minutes or until tender. Sprinkle with the parsley just before serving.

White Sauce

Thin
1 tablespoon Butter
1/4 teaspoon Salt
1 tablespoon Flour
1 cup Milk
Medium
2 tablespoons Butter
1/4 teaspoon Salt

2 tablespoons Flour
1 cup Milk
Thick
3 tablespoons Butter
1/4 teaspoon Salt
4 tablespoons Flour
1 cup Milk

Melt the butter in a small saucepan. Remove from heat and add the flour. Stir with a whisk until well blended. Add the salt and milk and return to a medium heat. Stir continually until thickened.

Cranberry Sauce

I have never really liked cranberry sauce. That was because our family always took it straight out of the can, sliced, and served. I made this recipe one year for my family and then worked up the nerve to try it myself. I like it—I like it.

2 cups Sugar   2 cups Water
1 lb (4 cups) Cranberries

Dissolve sugar into the water in a large saucepan. Heat to boiling. Boil for five minutes. Add the cranberries and simmer for fifteen minutes or until a drop jells on a cold plate. Pour into a four-cup mold. Chill until firm. (This takes a little longer, but I pour it through a fine strainer. I use a spoon to grind the berries and get the juice out.)

Raisin Sauce

This is a very nice sauce for your favorite ham. It is a little more complex than a regular raisin sauce. However, it is well worth the effort.

1/2 cup chopped Raisins   1 tablespoon Worcestershire
1/2 cup Water   Sauce
2 tablespoons Butter   3 tablespoons Red Wine Vine-
few drops of Tabasco Sauce   gar
pinch of Mace   dash of Salt and Pepper
1 cup Sugar   1/4 cup Red Currant Jelly

Mix the water and sugar in a saucepan and boil for five minutes. Add the remaining ingredients and simmer until the jelly is dissolved. Serve in your favorite gravy boat.

Summer Sandwich Loaf

Different salads are the main ingredient to this dish. Because of this, it does take some time to prepare this dish. I like to take it along when invited to a summer pot luck or I'm having guests over for lunch on a hot summer day. This sandwich really goes well with a small bowl of Gazpacho (cold tomato soup).

1 loaf of <u>unsliced</u> Bread
1/2 cup grated American Cheese
1/2 small Onion
8 slices Bacon, cooked and crumbled
3 tablespoons Mayonnaise

1 cup cooked, finely ground Chicken
1/2 cup minced Celery

1/4 cup Cream Cheese, softened
1/4 cup chopped Almonds
1 cup shredded Lettuce

1/4 cup Cream Cheese, softened
1/2 cup chopped Radishes
1/4 cup chopped Cucumber
1 8-oz package Cream Cheese, softened
Milk

Remove the crust from all around the loaf of bread. Carefully cut the loaf in half lengthwise, and then each half again in half lengthwise (four long slices). Place your first slice of bread on the platter that you are going to use to serve on. Spoon your mixture of cheese and bacon, onion and mayonnaise onto the bread, spreading to all edges. Cover with the next slice of bread. Spoon and spread the chicken and lettuce mixture as before. Cover with the third slice of bread. Top with cucumber and radish mixture. Place the last slice of bread on top and frost the whole thing with the last of the cream cheese that has been whipped with just enough milk to give it the consistency of frosting. Garnish as you like. I like curled cucumber slices all around the bottom edge and crumbled bacon and parsley flakes on top. Chill for at least an hour. Slice crosswise to serve.

Gravy (any flavor)

I have heard horror stories about gravies made for a wonderful dish. Then the gravy comes out lumpy, too thick, too runny or just God awful. This is probably the easiest, accident-proof gravy I have found. I love the praise from guests for this gravy and I have to date never given this recipe to anyone. Your guests will love it.

4 tablespoons Butter
2 cups hot Water

1 10 3/4-oz can Cream of
   Chicken Soup
4 tablespoons Flour
4 Chicken Bouillon cubes

Melt the bouillon cubes in the hot water until completely dissolved. In a saucepan, melt the butter and remove from heat. Mix in the flour until completely smooth. Add the bouillon broth and return to heat. Cook over a medium heat until thickened, stirring constantly. Add the cream of chicken soup. Heat completely and serve. You can use this recipe for pretty much all poultry dishes. (Hot turkey sandwiches—WONDERFUL!) If you are making a beef dish, you can still use this recipe because you can substitute beef bouillon cubes and cream of mushroom or cream of celery soup. You can also leave the soup out all together for a clearer gravy, as for hot beef sandwiches.

Kitchen Tips

- Sour milk? Add 1 tablespoon of vinegar or lemon juice to one cup of milk. Let stand for five minutes.
- To hold the egg whites together when poaching them, add a few drops of vinegar or lemon juice to the boiling water.
- If you need to measure less than one cup of shortening, pour cold water into a measuring cup and add the shortening. If 1/4 cup shortening is needed, pour 3/4 cup of cold water into the cup and then add enough shortening to equal one cup. Pour off the water.
- To bring life back to hard brown sugar, put the brown sugar into a plastic container and place half an apple in with it. Seal tightly.
- Save money on buying cooking oil. If you look in the beauty department in some department stores, you will find small spray bottles. They are usually less than a dollar. I washed one really well, filled it with vegetable oil, set it on the spray setting. It works great when you need to spray pans or baking sheets.
- Another pan grease saver. Mix 1/2 cup shortening and 1/4 cup flour into a smooth paste. Store in a small sealed container. When needed, spread the paste thinly on your pans.
- If you want to peel oranges or grapefruit fast and easy, let them stand in boiling water for about eight minutes before peeling.
- To keep lemons or limes fresh, place them in a glass jar filled with water and seal tightly.
- No more wrinkled skins on baked apples. Make a few slits before baking.
- Keep the skins on baked potatoes soft and tender. Put butter in your hands and cover the potato skins with it before baking.
- Freshen day-old dinner rolls. Place them in a paper bag and close with a twist top. Put them in an oven heated to 400 degrees for fifteen minutes.
- If you do not want your pie crust to shrink, put the pastry in the pie pan without stretching and set aside for at least five minutes.
- Vegetable stains on your hands? Rub them together with a slice of lemon.
- If your carrots, potatoes, or lettuce are a bit wilted, let stand in very cold salted water before using.
- If you want to skin a tomato fast and easy, stick a fork through the stem end, dip into boiling water, and then into cold water. Break skin at blossom end and peel the skin back.
- For rice that is whiter and more fluffy, add one teaspoon lemon juice to each quart of water while cooking.

107

- Add more flavor to homemade doughnuts. Place a couple of whole cloves or a stick of cinnamon in the oil while frying.
- If you want to open sealed jars easier, place the jar upside down in hot water for a few minutes.
- To remove the odor from jars or bottles, fill the jar half full with water and a tablespoon of dry mustard, seal, and shake well. Let sit for several hours.
- If you want keep a bowl from slipping all over your work space, set the bowl on a wet paper towel.
- If you are entertaining and you are serving a vodka or fruit flavored liquor, serve the bottle embedded in ice. Place the bottle in a large empty can or a half-gallon milk carton. Fill with cold water and freeze. Run the container under water and pull out the ice with the bottle. Slightly sculpt the ice with a pointed knife to give it some ridges and roughness. Keep frozen. When you are ready to serve, wrap a folded cloth napkin around the ice and secure with a knot.